Magical
Herbalism

Once, Witches Were the Keepers of the Secrets of the Earth

Witches knew the magical properties of the simple herbs that grew by fast-running streams, in verdant meadows, and high on lonely cliffs. As centuries passed and the world became mechanized, much of the old lore was forgotten.

Today, we are experiencing a resurgence of earth awareness and a reconnection with the natural world. The lost knowledge of herbal powers and correspondences is being rediscovered. This guidebook to the art and practice of magical herbalism will take you into the province of the witch and her kin—and teach you how to use this ancient, natural magic to better your life, and the lives of those you love.

About the Author

Scott Cunningham practiced elemental magic for more than twenty years. He was the author of more than thirty books, both fiction and nonfiction. Cunningham's books reflect a broad range of interests within the New Age sphere, where he was highly regarded. He passed from this life on March 28, 1993, after a long illness.

The Secret Craft of the Wise

Magical HERBALISM

SCOTT CUNNINGHAM

Llewellyn Publications
Woodbury, Minnesota

THIRD EDITION
Seventh Printing, 2010
First edition, two printings
Second edition, fifteen printings

Book design and editing by Kimberly Nightingale
Herbal safety editing by Melissa Mierva
Cover art © 2001 by Robert M. Place   FR
Cover design by Gavin Dayton Duffy

Library of Congress Cataloging-in-Publication Data
Cunningham, Scott, 1956–1993
  Magical herbalism.
  1. Magic. 2. Herbs. I. Title. II. Series.
  BF1623.P5C87   1986   133.4'4   83-80172
  ISBN 13: 978-0-87542-120-9
  ISBN 10: 0-87542-120-2

Llewellyn Worldwide does not participate in, endorse, or have any authority or responsibility concerning private business transactions between our authors and the public.

All mail addressed to the author is forwarded but the publisher cannot, unless specifically instructed by the author, give out an address or phone number.

Any Internet references contained in this work are current at publication time, but the publisher cannot guarantee that a specific location will continue to be maintained. Please refer to the publisher's website for links to authors' websites and other sources.

The old-fashioned remedies in this book are historical references used for teaching purposes only. The recipes are not for commercial use or profit. The contents are not meant to diagnose, treat, prescribe, or substitute consultation with a licensed healthcare professional.

Llewellyn Publications
A Division of Llewellyn Worldwide, Ltd.
2143 Wooddale Drive, Dept. 978-0-87542-120-9
Woodbury, MN 55125-2989, U.S.A.
www.llewellyn.com
Llewellyn is a registered trademark of Llewellyn Worldwide, Ltd.
Printed in the United States of America

Other Books by Scott Cunningham

The Complete Book of Incense, Oils & Brews

Cunningham's Encyclopedia of Crystal, Gem
    & Metal Magic

Cunningham's Encyclopedia of Magical Herbs

Dreaming the Divine

Earth, Air, Fire & Water

Earth Power

Hawaiian Magic & Spirituality

Living Wicca

Magical Aromatherapy

The Magical Household (with David Harrington)

Spell Crafts (with David Harrington)

The Truth About Herb Magic

The Truth About Witchcraft Today

Wicca

Biography

Whispers of the Moon
    (written by David Harrington and deTraci Regula)

Video

Herb Magic

*To the countless Witches—wise men and women—
who, down through the ages, have innovated,
perfected, and preserved these secrets*

Contents

Introduction   xv

Herbal magic—the ancient lore of the wise men and
women who lived in harmony with the earth in times
gone by is today being revived as people once again
seek to live healthy and natural lives. It is one of the
easiest and most enjoyable methods for finding your
earth roots, and gaining the power that is inherent in
nature herself.

PART ONE: Preparations

1 ⁓ Tools of the Magical Herbalist   3

The basic ritual equipment needed to practice magical
herbalism such as the magic knife, mortar and pestle,
censer, candles, etc., are all easily obtained or made, and
their preparation and use is enjoyable and satisfying.

2 ⁓ Magic—A Short Primer   13

Magic . . . "is the use of powers that reside within us
and the natural objects of our world to cause change."
Here are the basic principles and practical, simple techniques you need to know in order to do easy herbal
magic in your own home.

**3 ⁓ Identifying, Gathering, Drying,
    and Storing Herbs**   31

While sources of supply for the herbs you need are
given later, this chapter provides complete instructions
for the gathering and drying of wild herbs, and for
growing your own both outdoors and indoors.

4 ◆§ The Language of Magical Herbalism · 39

A short dictionary of magic and Witchcraft, and of the herbal craft, adds to understanding as well as enjoyment. Many of these words are part of the old Witches' tongue.

PART TWO: Herbal Secrets

5 ◆§ Protection · 49

Many herbs are blessed with protective vibrations, and this chapter details the use of herbs for these purposes. A short exorcism (purification) ritual for a new home or apartment is included.

6 ◆§ Divination · 59

The power to divine, to see the future through dreams, or with the aid of cards, or crystals, or visions, can be aided and strengthened through the use of herbal techniques involving incenses, oils, teas, sachets, and herbal pillows.

7 ◆§ Healing · 69

Healing incenses and rituals using the magical (rather than the medicinal) properties of herbs are explained. Here are ancient chants, amulets, and occult remedies.

8 ◆§ Love · 81

The occult powers of herbs can be used to win (or brush off) a love, inspire romance, and raise the sexual passions. Here are recipes for love incenses, sachets and spells, marriage and fertility charms, and for sexual prowess.

9 ❧ Herbs of the Elements and Magical
Fluid Condensers   87

The fluid condenser captures, concentrates, and stores
the innate power of herbs. Here are step-by-step instructions in the making and use of these powerful aids
with specific application and guidance to the herbs of
choice.

10 ❧ Scented Oils and Perfumes   99

All herbal magic works through vibrations and scent.
Here you learn to use oils scented with herbs, a tech-
nique that concentrates the powers of the herb as well
as directly influencing the mind and emotions through
scent to trigger various centers in the brain. Here are
recipes for love, power, protection, divination, health,
and much more. Includes the famous satyr oil, Venus
oil, and four winds oil, as well as an extensive guide to
the magical powers of easily made or available scented
oils, from acacia and all-spice to wisteria and ylang-
ylang.

11 ❧ Incenses   119

How to make your own incenses, and how to use
them for magical purposes. Includes special recipes
that aid meditation, Egyptian magic, lunar rituals,
prosperity, purification, etc.

12 ❧ Amulets   131

A collection of traditional charms and amulets.

13 ◆§ Witch's Herbal **135**

An alphabetical listing of 118 major magical herbs—
with astrological and planetary rulership, vibrational
level, folk as well as technical names, magical powers,
and special uses.

PART THREE: The Magic Garden

14 ◆§ Your Herbal Garden **213**

Yes, you can grow your own magical herbs! And they are
the more magical for your doing so. Here are instructions for the selection of the plants and seeds, the principles of magically preparing the land and of magical
gardening, and of giving your garden magical protection.

Appendices

**1 ◆§ The Magical Names of Herbs, Flowers,
Trees, and Roots** **231**

The romance of the secret and magical names as used
by the ancient herbalists and Witches. Here is the real
meaning of "eye of newt," "toe of frog," "hat's wings,"
etc., and a glossary to help the student and researcher.

2 ◆§ Baneful Herbs and Flying Ointments **235**

The magical and psychic uses of belladonna, *Amanita
muscaria,* hellebore, hemlock, hemp, henbane, and the
famous flying ointment used to induce astral projection.

3 ❧ **Sources for Herbs and Oils**   **243**
A short directory of names and addresses.

4 ❧ **Herbal Redes**   **245**
A collection of wise sayings concerning herbs that
every herbalist should know.

     Bibliography   **249**

     Index   **255**

Introduction

In centuries past, when the nightmares we know of as cities had yet to be born, we lived in harmony with the earth and used her treasures wisely. Many knew the old magics of herbs and plants.

Knowledge was passed down from one generation to another, and so the lore was widely circulated and used. Most country folk knew one herb that was a powerful protection against evil, or a certain flower that produced prophetic dreams, and perhaps a sure-fire love charm or two.

Witches had their own intricate operations of herbal magic, as did the magicians and alchemists. Soon a body of magical knowledge accumulated surrounding the simple herbs that grew by fast-running streams, in verdant meadows, and high on lonely cliffs.

Many of our ancestors, however, looked to the stars, away from the earth, and dreamed of greater things. In racing toward mechanized perfection, humanity became orphaned of the earth, and much of the old lore was forgotten.

Fortunately, it was not lost completely. Witches became the keepers of the secrets of the earth; thus, they were looked upon with fear by those who had already turned their backs on the Old Ways. Terror and hatred forced the Witches into hiding, and for centuries their secrets remained untouched.

When the old Witches died, many of their secrets died with them, for as the centuries passed there were fewer and fewer who cared to learn the ancient arts of magic.

Today we are experiencing a resurgence of earth awareness. Ecological organizations prosper. Recycling is a booming business. People are turning away from chemicals and artificially preserved foods to more healthy fare.

Herbs long unadored have once again come into their own. But aside from hints and speculation, the magical art of herbalism has largely been left unexplored and unexplained.

This book is an attempt to fill this gap in herbal knowledge. Though these instructions have long been the province of the Witch and her kin, all that is required to successfully practice magical herbalism is an earnest desire to better your life, and the lives of those you know and love.

This is a complete and practical guide. No esoteric, misty treatise, it should serve well as an introduction to herbal magic—the postive aspects of herbal magic. Aside from an appendix that discusses the use of baneful herbs, no poisoning, cursing, controlling, compelling, binding, or otherwise evil magical information is contained herein, for such practices have no place in the divine magic of the herbalist.

In magic, especially herbal magic, an herb is a plant prized for its vibrations, or energies. Thus, the herbs of this book include seaweeds, cacti, trees, fruits, and flowers that one might not normally consider to be herbs.

Recent advances in science have enabled us to photographically record these vibrations through the use of Kirilian photography. Thus, science once again vindicates magic.

There are Witches still, who walk unshod upon the earth and listen to the murmurings of the trees and garland themselves with sacred herbs while the Moon watches far above.

What remains of their fabled lore is fragmented; a patchwork of beliefs, knowledge, and rituals. These remnants, however, are just as effective today as when they were born in a more magical age.

Herbal magic is one of the easiest, safest, and most joyous methods of reestablishing earth roots, of returning to a healthy and natural life. It touches the essence of life itself with simple rituals and few props.

The magic is in the herbs—and in you. Herbal magic is a cooperation between plant and human, between earth and heaven, between microcosm and macrocosm—a union of energies forged to produce change by methods that outsiders view as being supernatural.

That these ways are far more natural, far older than the computerized religions and prefabricated societal values of today's world may escape many, but that is the way of magic. It is not for everybody.

There are no vows to swear, no groups to join, and no demons to worship. And, though there are a few simple rules to follow that ensure best results, the magic can be as simple or complex as you wish.

This is a book of power, of the magic of herbs. The knowledge contained within it has been preserved so that we may better our lives.

Use it with love.

PART ONE

Preparations

1

Tools of the Magical Herbalist

All professions and avocations have their own tools of the trade, and magic is no exception. Tools are the objects with which change is wrought. Magic is sometimes defined as "change wrought by psychic means," so the tools used in magic should be carefully selected, made, or prepared in order to carry out their function.

The most important tool used in herbal magic is the magic knife. This is a first cousin to the athame, the Witches' mystic knife that is used in religious and magical rites by initiates of the Old Religion. The basic difference between the athame and the magic knife is that the former is used purely for symbolic or energy directing purposes, whereas the magic knife is used for cutting herbs, thread, cloth, etc., as well as for banishing, exorcising, enchanting, and so on.

To make your knife, find one with a wooden handle and steel blade that fits comfortably in your hand. Be sure that it is new and clean. Buy it without haggling over the price. Wrap it up in a clean, white cotton or linen cloth and hide it where it will not be disturbed until the next Full Moon. (The purchase of a yearly astrological guide, such as the annual Llewellyn's *Moon Sign Book,* is a great help to the magical herbalist. See the bibliography.)

On this night, just after sunset, go to a lonely, wild place, far out in the countryside. Ideally, there will be a stream running nearby, a small hill, and complete privacy. Clear an area on the ground and gather a little wood to make a fire. Lay a book of matches beside the wood. If no stream is available, bring a bowl of silver or pewter and fill it with spring water. If you cannot leave the city, perform the rite in your garden or, failing even this, in your home, using a flowerpot filled with earth, a fireplace or candle, and the bowl of water.

Now, finding a quiet spot, bury the knife in the earth up to the hilt, so that the handle points to the sky. Kneel before it. Placing your hands upon the ground on either side of it, facing north, say these words:

> *I conjure thee, O knife of steel,*
> *by the powers of the earth,*
> *that thou shalt be of service to me*
> *in the magical art of herbalism.*

Count to thirty slowly, then grip the handle in your strong hand (the one you write with) and pull it from the earth.

Now walk to the highest nearby spot, a hill, or rock, and climb to the top. Holding your knife up to the sky and facing east, say these words:

I conjure thee, O knife of steel,
by the power of the winds,
that thou shalt be of service to me
in the magical art of herbalism.

Next, build a small fire of the wood and light it. Then, facing south, thrust the blade amidst the flames and say these or similar words:

I conjure thee, O knife of steel,
by the powers of the flames,
that thou shalt be of service to me
in the magical art of herbalism.

Next, walk to the stream and dip the blade into the running water (or, the filled bowl). Say these or like words as you face west:

I conjure thee, O knife of steel,
by the powers of the water,
that thou shalt be of service to me
in the magical art of herbalism.

Now wrap the knife in a clean, white cloth, quench the fire with the water from the stream or bowl, and return home. Keep the knife safely hidden until needed. With this knife you will cut all herbs, flowers, plants, seeds, cords, cloth; whatever is needed for your magical practices. Keep it sharp and shiny.

The next most important tool is the magic wand. As the magic knife is used to consecrate, cut, and perform the more lowly operations, the wand is an instrument of invocation, of invitation.

The construction of the wand should take place during the Waxing Moon and at night. The actual type of wood used depends on the interests of the magician.

For instance, hazel or elder wood is most often used for magic wands, as these trees make excellent all-purpose wands.

Some magical herbalists, however, are more specialized, and have one wand for every type of magic they perform. Thus, the following list:

Love magic—Apple

Healing magic—Ash

Exorcisms—Elder

Prosperity—Fir

Protection—Rowan

Purification and blessings—Birch

Moon magic and wishing magic—Willow

For fertility magic, an oak wand topped with an acorn (or one made of fir, tipped with a pine cone) is often used.

As the wood must be obtained from a living tree, you may not be able to obtain the specific type you desire. But fortunately, most trees, especially fruit trees, will work adequately in magic.

During the construction of the magic wand you will use your magic knife.

Take a purification bath (see next chapter) and then dress in clean, plain clothes or a robe. Go to the tree. Walk thrice around its trunk clockwise, pointing your knife at the tree, and saying words similar to these:

O great tree,
O strong tree,
I ask thee to give me of your wood
to further me in the magical art of herbalism.
Thou shalt grow strong by my stroke;
stronger and taller,
O great tree!

Finished, select an appropriate branch, straight with few leaves or twigs growing out of it. A length of perhaps fifteen inches is sufficient to allow shaping and sanding, and a width of not less than one-half inch is fine.

With your magic knife cut the branch tenderly, whispering your thanks to the tree. Tie a red bow around the trunk or bury an offering of bread, wine, or a precious stone at its base.

After returning home, remove all extraneous growth from the main shaft. Sand with a fairly coarse sandpaper to remove the bark, then shift to a lighter paper to smooth it. Then wipe with a dry cloth to remove the wood dust. Now anoint a cloth with pure frankincense or sandalwood oil and rub the wand well with this. Put away in a dark place, wrapped in a yellow cloth, for seven days. On this night, take it out and lay it upon the bare earth. Touch the point of your magic knife to the wand, saying these or similar words of like meaning:

I consecrate thee,
O wand of (type of tree),
by the virtues of the earth, air, fire, and water,
that thou shalt truly be a magical wand,
possessed of bounteous powers and uses.
By this sign thou shalt be an aid and succour to me.

Now, setting the knife aside (or, sliding it in your belt or sheath) hold the wand in your strong hand. Grasp firmly. Now invoke any god you worship. Repeat the invocation in each of the four directions (you do not have to be exact in these; it is okay to guess).

Many feel more comfortable working magic in the name of a god or goddess. Although magic is nonreligious, it is not nonspiritual (on the contrary, it is at the heart and soul of every religious philosophy). If you feel more at ease flavoring your magic with religion, by all means do so. This is where the wand will come in hand, on calling upon your gods to witness your rites or to charge them with extra power.

Raise the wand aloft in your strong hand when invoking or praying to deities, calling upon the powers of earth, air, fire, and water, or when dealing with any nonhuman entity.

Here is a list of the other tools you will need:

Mortar and pestle. Such sets are useful for grinding up and mixing herbs, or crushing flowers and bark and composing incenses and powders. They are available in most hardware, herb, and department stores, the latter usually keeping them in the cookware section.

They are available in a wide variety of materials and sizes. The glass and ceramic mortars, while favored by some for their nonmetallic content, can break if not used with a gentle hand. The wooden models tend to absorb odors and can splinter or chip. The metal or stone ones seem to be the best for general working.

There is no consecration ceremony necessary for your mortar and pestle. Simply wash them well (before the first use) and set to dry before a fire.

A two-quart (or larger) glass, enamelled or otherwise nonmetallic and heat-resistant pot, in which to brew infusions, condensers, and other magical liquids. It should have a heat-resistant handle, so that you will not burn your hands or have to use potholders. It must also come equipped with a tight fitting glass or ceramic lid, to contain steam and essential oils while processing herbs.

A source of flame. Much of the magic in magical herbalism is enhanced by the use of fire. Old instructions specify a flame for heating purposes. Thus, a gas stove, a fireplace, a propane camping stove, even a can of Sterno will do. If you are fortunate enough to have a fireplace, construct a means to hang a pot over the fire for heating purposes. Naturally, if your source of fire is in the room in which you will be practicing your magic, it will be to your benefit.

Keep a large stock of candles and holders. The tapers are fine for most rituals. Beeswax is traditional, but the ordinary stearin variety will do as well and is less expensive. Have on hand a good selection of colors for the following uses:

Pink—Love and affection

Green—Prosperity and fertility

Red—Passion and vitality

Blue—Healing and peace

Yellow—Mental powers, intellectualism

Purple—Boost your own magical powers

White—General work and blessings

Brown—Making magic for animals

Black—Banishing illnesses, breaking hexes, exorcisms

A censer, or something to burn incense in. A small dish, filled one-third with clean sand, will do. Check religious supply stores to find one of the more ornate models, or try antique shops. The first time it is used, burn pure frankincense or rosemary in it to purify it.

Charcoal blocks, upon which to burn the incense. These are available from herb shops, occult stores, and religious supply outlets. They are also available by mail (see appendix 3). The quick-lighting kind are recommended.

Pure, virgin olive oil. This is required in many spells.

Sea salt is sometimes necessary for certain rituals. It is available in health food stores.

Spring water. If there is a spring nearby, fill gallon jugs and cork well to ensure a continuing supply. If not, bottled spring water is acceptable.

Needles and supplies, a wide selection of colored threads, pins, yarn, cheesecloth, muslin, and other natural fabrics for making sachets, amulets, and so on.

An eye-dropper for blending oils.

A dip pen (no ballpoints) and black, red, and green ink.

And of course, **a large supply of herbs.** A basic beginning selection might include rosemary, vervain, bay laurel, yarrow, rue, frankincense, cinnamon, eucalyptus, and mistletoe. These are useful in a wide variety of spells and are fairly easily obtainable.

Naturally, your stock of herbs will grow with time, when you begin collecting your own and purchasing ingredients for specific rituals.

© Robin Wood 1986

2

Magic— A Short Primer

Magic is the art of causing change by means commonly supposed to be supernatural. The methods of magic are varied, each catering to a certain climate or level of intellectual development or imagination. Simple or ceremonial, Christian or Cabalistic, all magical practices have survived because of one basic reason: they work.

That science has not yet uncovered all the secrets of the universe is questioned by few. Magic is simply the use of powers not yet recognized by science. Hypnosis, for example, was a part of the occult tradition for centuries; once it was investigated, and then recognized by the scientific community, it lost most of its mystical, supernatural tone.

Magic is, despite claims to the contrary, a very natural art. It is the use of powers that reside within us and the natural objects of our world to cause change. Magical herbalism is the use of herbs for magic.

Following is a summing-up of magical thought, condensed into simple, universal ideas. All magic in this book should be performed with these in mind.

Basic Principles of Magic

Magic is a natural science, with known avenues, byways, and borders, as well as principles and laws. It is well to stay within the explored territories and to observe these laws.

Harm none. It is an old Witch tradition that whatever you do will be returned to you three-fold, "three times ill or three times good." Thus, harmful magic extracts a very high price. This rule applies to one's self as well. Do not do anything (magically speaking) that will harm you.

If you wish to break up a love affair, kill your wife, or cause tons of money to fall out of a bank vault into your hands, look elsewhere. Such magic is never worth the consequences.

Magic requires effort. You will get out of it precisely what you put into it in terms of time, energy, and attention to ritual. If a spell requires you to travel to three different streams, climb a hill, or make a green candle, do it.

These are rituals and there are sound magical and psychological reasons for ritual. Ritual strengthens, defines, and directs magical power. Leave the ritual out and the magic will falter. Some budding magical herbalists turn away with a sigh on discovering that magic is hard work. There are no two ways about it—anything worth doing at all is worth doing well. Shortcuts rarely produce satisfactory results and can even be dangerous!

Magic is not instantaneous. Some rituals produce quick results but most work over a period of time. This is especially true concerning herbal magic. There are rituals that must be repeated several days in a row to be effective at all. Herbal magic works on vibrations and vibrations can be altered to your own purposes. But Stonehenge was not built in a day. A prosperity ritual does not instantly materialize a thousand-dollar bill in your pocket. Usually, the fruits of magic will manifest in a perfectly "normal" way, as if they were not magically induced. While this fuels the skeptic's fire, think of it as a manifestation of the naturalness of magic.

Magic should never be performed for pay, for money tempts the magician to use the art for evil or frivolous means. If a friend hears of your magic and wants you to perform a spell or sew up a sachet for them, and they offer to pay for it, do not accept the money. It is just, however, to ask them to purchase the ingredients necessary for the spell.

Magic should never be used to play up one's vanity or pride. When magic becomes an ego trip it will soon lose its effectiveness.

Magic can be worked for your own gain, but only if you are certain that this will not harm others.

Magic deserves a sound investment. This may mean purchasing tools, herbs, candles or whatever you will need in your art. Most of these items can be made if you are handy at forging, gardening, chandlery, and so on. It is fine to purchase your tools, though. It is one of the oldest of magical laws that you should never haggle or try to lower the price of anything that is bought for use in magic. Also, use new candles for each spell. If one spell is repeated over several nights, the same candles are used. But when a new spell is begun it is best to get new candles.

If you have regular altar candles burning in addition to your own special spell candle, these can be used several times without needing to be changed, as their basic function is to provide illumination.

Do not throw away half-burned candles. Store them to melt down at a later time to make new candles. (Your public library should have some excellent works on candle making.)

Magic is a divine art, and so the magician and all tools should be clean and pure. Keep your thoughts pure and true to your purpose at all times in magic. A wandering mind nullifies the effects of magic, while a disciplined, concentrating one will boost it.

Magic is not always serious or solemn. It is a joyous celebration and merging with the lifeforce.

Laughter and singing, poetry, and ecstatic dance can be incorporated into your rituals—whatever is within your particular talents. There are no hard and fast rules for the exact procedure and nature of rituals, so spontaneity should be encouraged and welcomed.

Magic is intent. Witches are taught that the most important factor in magic-making is the intent. You must firmly visualize in your mind's eye the thing you wish to have happen. See it as if it has already taken place, or been brought into manifestation. This adds to the power of your magic.

In herbal magic the magician is working with two powers: those of the herbs themselves and with his or her own personal energies. Thus, the magic can sometimes be magic with the innate powers of the herbs alone, and this is one of the great advantages of herbal magic. But the addition of one's own powers acts as a booster and charger to make these powers stronger, to give them a purpose and intent, a kind of focusing and funnelling of their powers to one specific purpose. This is the value of intent.

This is also achieved to a certain degree by the act of enchanting. This means, simply, "singing to." When cutting herbs, sewing up sachets, or making other herbal magics, a short rune or poem is often repeated in a sing-song or monotone manner. In these poems the intent is vividly described, and this helps to reinforce the image in the mind, as well as to channel the energies of the herbs themselves. Thus, the herbs are told in no uncertain terms what they are supposed to do. The real effect of this lies not in the words spoken, but in the intent. The words simply reinforce the mind-picture.

Magic is faith. If you have no faith in your magic or within yourself, you will not get positive results. Believe!

Magic is love. Without love, the magician is powerless. Love is the strongest emotion in the universe. All magic should be performed out of love for one's self, family, friends, neighbors, country, planet, gods. It is the spark that sets the fuel of magic bursting forth.

This book is nondenominational; it has been structured so that it can be used within any religious tradition. Religious magic is simply that clone in the name of (or with the help of) a god, goddess, or both.

In sum, magic is the natural, loving practice that taps the limitless powers of life to cause beneficial changes to ourselves, our friends and loved ones, our Earth, and even beyond.

Following are a number of short sections covering some specifics of magical procedure dealing with such topics as the best time to perform magic, the place, preparation for ritual, and a number of shorter suggestions and tips.

The Place

The best places for performing magic are hidden, secret areas far from cities and highways. Desolate and uninhabited regions are the most traditional, such as forests, ruins, mountain tops, caves, deserts; beside lightning-struck trees, earthworks, standing stones, and ancient monuments; on shining seashores, the banks of great streams, or at a crossroads where three rivers meet. If you elect to perform your magic in these places, be sure that you will be safe from accidental discovery.

Magic being practical, however, your own home can be used with good results, provided that care is taken against the sudden intrusion of outsiders, and the area is ritually purified and cleansed.

A bedroom is perhaps the most-used place, for that is the room in which we spend most of our time. Most powerful, however, is a whole room reserved exclusively for the arts of magic. There, you can house your herb cabinet, magical tools and books, dry your herbs and roots, and set up a permanent altar. Setting aside one room for magic alone is ideal, for the vibrations inside will become attuned to your workings, and will be a source of added power.

If you decide to work indoors, every week or so burn frankincense in your "magic room." This clears it of negative vibrations.

The Time

The following section on when to perform magical operations includes traditional information, such as has been used for many hundreds of years. It has been used to good advantage, but that does not make it necessary or even desirable.

Magic, all magic, should be practical. In the end it does not matter what day of the week it is, or phase of the Moon, or hour of the day. What is important is the intent that the magician has in performing an act of magic. If the energies are there (from the herbs and from yourself) nothing else matters unless you believe it does.

True, the energies run in cycles. But we must remember we are tapping a universal power source through our magic. Our own bodies and the herbs we use are links with this great power. Since it is universal, it is all-encompassing. Where our Moon ebbs, another flows. All balances out in the end, so there is no deficit or credit; the energies remain constant, stable, strong.

The lifeforce of the universe, which powers our souls, gave birth to the planets, and nourishes the green things of the Earth, is timeless and eternal. Since all is linked through the lifeforce, this power can be tapped at all times, no matter what the season, or where Venus rides in the sky.

So these systems are simply traditional, to be used if you wish. Bear in mind, please, that they are unnecessary. Systems are there to aid us, but we should not enslave ourselves to them.

The best time to perform magic is at night. The Sun has set, the Moon rides high in the sky, men and women drift off to sleep. The pace of the city slows to a crawl, and all is hushed and still.

Midnight is known as the "witching hour" because it is the ideal time to perform magic.

Look to the Moon, too, to guide your actions. The Waxing Moon is the proper time to perform favorable magic (fertility, love, protection, prosperity, good health). The Waning Moon is ideal for rituals involving destruction of old habits, banishing curses and hexes, and removing illness and disease.

Even the day of the week and the hour of the day can be important. Here are charts that will enable you to choose the appropriate days and hours for your magical operations.

Sunday is ruled by the Sun

Monday is ruled by the Moon

Tuesday is ruled by Mars

Wednesday is ruled by Mercury

Thursday is ruled by Jupiter

Friday is ruled by Venus

Saturday is ruled by Saturn

The Sun rules all operations involving employers, promotions, friendships, healing, divine power, labor, world leaders.

The Moon rules spells dealing with the home, family, agriculture, cooking, clairvoyance, medicine, dreams, the sea.

Mars rules all operations of conflict, hunting, surgery, lust, physical strength, courage, politics, debates, athletics, war, contests, competitions, rituals involving men.

Mercury rules rites involving studying, learning, teaching, divination, predictions, self-improvement, communications of every kind, the mind, celibacy.

Jupiter rules all rituals of wealth, poverty, monetary matters, legal matters, honors, luck, materialism, expansion.

Venus rules all operations of love, pleasure, art, music, incense and perfume composition, partnerships, rituals involving women.

Saturn rules those operations concerning buildings, the elderly, funerals, wills, reincarnation, destroying diseases and pests, terminations, and death.

This list can he extended indefinitely with serious thought and meditation.

Planetary Hours of the Night

	Sun.	Mon.	Tues.	Wed.	Thurs.	Fri.	Sat.
1	Jupiter	Venus	Saturn	Sun	Moon	Mars	Mercury
2	Mars	Mercury	Jupiter	Venus	Saturn	Sun	Moon
3	Sun	Moon	Mars	Mercury	Jupiter	Venus	Saturn
4	Venus	Saturn	Sun	Moon	Mars	Mercury	Jupiter
5	Mercury	Jupiter	Venus	Saturn	Sun	Moon	Mars
6	Moon	Mars	Mercury	Jupiter	Venus	Saturn	Sun
7	Saturn	Sun	Moon	Mars	Mercury	Jupiter	Venus
8	Jupiter	Venus	Saturn	Sun	Moon	Mars	Mercury
9	Mars	Mercury	Jupiter	Venus	Saturn	Sun	Moon
10	Sun	Moon	Mars	Mercury	Jupiter	Venus	Saturn
11	Venus	Saturn	Sun	Moon	Mars	Mercury	Jupiter
12	Mercury	Jupiter	Venus	Saturn	Sun	Moon	Mars

Note that this table is for hours of the night only. The actual length of these "hours" depends upon the period of time between sunset and sunrise the following day. To find the length of each hour, take the actual number of minutes between sunset and sunrise and then divide by twelve. This gives the number of minutes for each hour, the first hour beginning at sunset.

These lengthy calculations are not necessary, but are traditional. If you keep in mind the phase of the Moon and the day of the week and align them with your ritual, you will have positive results. Performing your magic in the planetary hour will not hurt, especially if you cannot wait for the correct day of the week.

Here is an example of how the charts can be used. Say you need a sum of money quickly to pay an unexpected bill. Prosperity rituals are ruled by Jupiter, so plan to do the ritual on Thursday during the third or tenth hour of the night, if possible. As you wish your money to increase, rather than decrease, be sure that this Thursday falls within the Waxing Moon.

You can follow the same procedure for every ritual. Find the correct day of the week, phase of the Moon, and hour (if you desire). In addition to Llewellyn's *Moon Sign Book* for determining the phase of the Moon, some students use *The Improved Perpetual Planetary Hour Book* by Llewellyn George that lists the local times of the planetary hours day and night throughout the year for most locations in the United States, (see Bibliography).

The Altar

Some call this the altar, some the working space. An altar is the table that is the center of a religious ceremony. Whether or not your magic is religiously oriented is beside the point, however. For simplicity's sake the working place will be referred to as the altar throughout this book.

You will need a flat surface, about two feet square, upon which to work your magic. While working outdoors, old tree stumps, flat-topped rocks, or cleared sections of the ground are often used. For in-home use, the purchase of a small, low table is perhaps necessary, although a coffee table or nightstand will do.

Most altars are erected facing north. North was anciently believed to be the direction from which power flowed. North is the realm of herbal magic, of familiars, and of midnight. Though some Witches put their altars facing east, in honor of the Sun and Moon that rise there, better results will come about if it is placed facing north.

Take a square of white cloth and lay it on your altar. It should drape to the floor. Place two candles in identical candlesticks on the two corners farthest away from you. Between them place your incense burner. Before this set down your magic knife, and to the right of this place a small jar of incense (for general working, use frankincense). Place any other needed objects (herbs, pieces of cloth, needles and thread, oils) to the left of the censer. Be sure the objects on the altar form a balanced picture.

If you will be incorporating your religion in magic, you would want to place an image or symbol of your religion on the altar, behind the censer, between the candles. A crucifix or a statue of a god or goddess works well.

Many Witches and magicians add a vase of fresh flowers and greens to give extra life to the altar. This is a particularly excellent idea, especially if you also insert a few sprigs of the herbs that are appropriate to the rite. For instance, a little rosemary gives added power to an altar set up for a rite of love.

Just prior to performing your first piece of magic on your new altar, fumigate the area with frankincense smoke. This is absolutely essential. If frankincense is not immediately available (most mail-order suppliers and religious supply shops carry it) burn rosemary leaves on your charcoal, as was the custom in ancient Greece, to purify the room.

Never forget that this is a natural magic that you are performing. It is too easy to get caught up in the little magical world of the magic room, and lose direct contact with the earth. Walk barefoot on the grass, among tall trees, and drink in the vibrations they give off.

Take trips to beaches and deserts, to rivers and other places of natural beauty and energy. The more you do this, the more you will be able to tap the hidden forces of nature.

Preparation for Magic

Make sure that you are quite alone in the house and that no one will be coming to visit you.

Shut off all heating and cooling devices. Take the phone off the hook. Close all curtains, shutters, or blinds. Lock all doors and windows so that you are perfectly secure and free from the fear of discovery. If you cannot be alone in the house, be sure that no one will bother you for a few hours. Tell the others to hold all your calls. Be adamant about this, as it is best to work magic without interruption.

It is not advisable to have friends present while working magic, as they are more often an inhibitor than a source of added power. Magic is best performed alone unless you and a friend are studying together and have found that you can pool your powers effectively.

The floor of the magic room should be freshly swept and mopped or vacuumed. If there is a fireplace near or in the room itself, light a fire, preferably oak, pine, holly, hazel, juniper, cedar, poplar, apple, or ash woods.

Tie up in a four-inch square piece of cheesecloth half a handful of the following mixture: equal parts of vervain, garden mint, basil, thyme, fennel, lavender, rosemary, hyssop, and valerian. This purification bath blend may be mixed together in advance and the sachets conveniently made up in advance. Keep them in an airtight jar until needed.

Light a white taper and take it with the sachet into the bathroom. Run a quarter-tubful of very warm water. Toss the sachet into the water and then step into it, placing the candle in a crystal holder. Relax in the bath for several minutes, squeezing the sachet so that the herbs release their scents and oils to the water. For added purification purposes, sprinkle a bit of sea salt into the water as well.

(*Note:* As valerian has a peculiarly strong odor, I usually add a bit more lavender and a lot less of the ground valerian root to the mixture. This imparts a more pleasant scent.)

Relax in the bath. Feel the tensions of everyday living slipping away from you. If you wish, use a natural soap to cleanse yourself physically while the sachet cleanses you psychically. When finished, dry quickly with a soft towel. Anoint yourself with a favorite perfume or cologne (or magical oil: see chapter 6), touching the soles of your feet, wrists, and forehead. Don a robe, regular clothes, or walk naked, holding the candle before you, into your magic room.

If you do not have a bathtub, boil two quarts water, remove from heat, and add a sachet. Cover this and let stand for about an hour. Then, take a shower and after the usual soaping pour the infusion onto your body.

This works fairly well. There is nothing like the magical bath, however!

Light the charcoal block with the candle and watch it sputter and spark into life. Then light the tapers, first right and then left, with the white taper. Silently blow out your purification bath taper and set aside in a safe place, to be used to begin every ritual. Pour a little incense on the charcoal and you are ready to begin to perform magic.

The use of magical dress is partly psychological, partly magical. When putting on a garment reserved for special occasions one becomes infused with the spirit of the moment. Also, a robe that is worn every time one performs magic will become infused with magical energy, thus strengthening your own each time you put it on. Magical herbalists favor green robes.

Ritual nudity is often used in magic as a symbol of purity, honesty, and mortality. It is an excellent way to contact the primal forces of nature which, after all, did not bring us into this world wearing clothing. In fact, many of the old rituals involving fertility and love specifically state that the celebrant be naked.

If a robe is not available and nudity is undesirable, wear clean clothes, preferably in the rich, earthy hues of browns and greens.

Choose the method that seems the most comfortable to you, for that is what is supremely important.

Herbal Numerology

The numbers 3, 7, and 9 are favored in herbal magic and often appear in lists of ingredients and repetitions of actions in spells and rituals. The multiples of these numbers are also favored.

Odd numbers are generally considered fortunate in magic; however, some old charms call for four ingredients, symbolizing the four elements, or directions, or winds.

Counting itself is a magical act. It lulls the mind into a semiconscious state. Often in herbal magic a period of time must elapse between two actions. When this needs to be done, either count heartbeats (a favorite practice of the Witches) or check a nearby clock.

Definitely do not wear a wristwatch, or interrupt meditation by looking at the clock. One of the small timers that rings a bell when a certain amount of time has passed might be a good investment.

Odds and Ends

Replace all sachets, amulets, and magic pillows every three months, for the power wanes with time.

Never do more than three pieces of magic a day. If you are doing two or more rituals, and one (or more) is for someone else, do your personal spell last.

When saying incantations, runes, or other spoken parts of spells, say them in a firm, clear voice. If you are afraid of being heard by neighbors, say the words slowly and quietly, with fierce concentration and conviction.

In herbal magic repetition means added power. It is fine to do a spell several times in order to give it added power. Always follow instructions carefully. It is fruitless to add extra herbs or to load up on one herb, thinking it will give it extra power.

Remember, it is not the quantity of the herbs, oils, incenses, or whatever that counts, but the quality. If you follow instructions carefully, the magic usually works.

If an herb is not available, substitute it with another of like properties, that also shares the same planetary and elemental rulers.

Keep a notebook of recipes, thoughts, and complete records of your spells, success/failure rates, etc. Also record all pertinent data, such as the phase of the Moon, astrological aspects (if you are trained in this field), Sun and Moon astrological houses, weather conditions (rain, fog, electrical storm), and so on. By studying this book every week or so, you can see how the weather and the Sun and Moon affect your magical performance. You might also want to record any dreams you have related to magic or other occult topics.

As stated before, wristwatches are definitely taboo within the magic room, as are hair pins, makeup, deodorants, shoes, socks, sandals, boots, and most kinds of metallic or plastic accessories. Jewelry such as necklaces, rings, and pendants are fine, especially if they are of magical designs (such as pentagrams, ankhs, or hexagrams), or if they are especially meaningful to you.

3

Identifying, Gathering, Drying, and Storing Herbs

We are fortunate today to be able to purchase many herbs in specialty shops or by mail. The Witch of the past had no such conveniences, and had to gather most of the herbs she used herself. Though store-bought herbs work well in magic (and are often imported from other countries, thus negating the possibility of personal collection) those that you have collected, dried, and enchanted yourself will be triply powerful.

Many of the herbs that grow wild in these lands came here with settlers and explorers. Colonists grew familiar herbs in their culinary gardens, and over the centuries these plants escaped and spread out across the land, so that dozens of the sacred herbs of Witchcraft and magic now grow wild in forests, near streams, and high in the mountains the entire length and breadth of the country.

Many bookstores sell "field guides" that are of immense help in properly identifying the herbs that grow in your

area. Such plants are classified in these books as wildflow-
ers, or simply wild plants. Get a good guide book and use
it when walking your surrounding countryside to scout
future sources of herbs.

When choosing sites for herb collection, make sure
they are far from highways, polluted rivers, and stagnant
water. Also, be certain that they have not been sprayed
with insecticides or other chemicals.

If you cannot positively identify an herb, pass it
over. Many plants are similar in appearance and can be
mistaken for ones that are harmful, even if not taken
internally.

Gathering

Herbs are magical substances, infused with the energy of
the Earth. Specific instructions detailing the proper collection procedures have been formulated over the years and
better results will be obtained if they are followed.

The Moon waxes and wanes, pulling with her the
seas of the Earth and producing its tides. So, too, does
this influence manifest in all living things, including
herbs. During the waxing of the Moon the vital energies
flow upward, into the leaves and stalks and flowers of
the plant. As the Moon wanes these energies travel to
the roots.

To obtain herbs that are highly energized, pick them
according to the Moon's phases. Leaves, flowers, and
seeds should be picked during the Waxing Moon, when
it is growing from New to Full. All root crops should be
picked during the Waning Moon, from Full to New.

As night is the Moon's domain, most herbs are picked after sunset on a clear, dry night. Some Witches pick each herb only during its own planetary hour, believing this gives the plants added power. The "Witch's Herbal" section of the book (Part Two, chapter 13) lists the most-used herbs and their planetary rulers. For more information on planetary hours see "Planetary Hours of the Night," page 22, in the last chapter.

Determine the appropriate night (taking into consideration the Moon and, if you wish, the planetary day and hour) for your herb collection. Fast for three hours prior to your departure, and gather together your magic knife, a cloth bag, and a piece of bread (homemade is best). It is not advisable to pick plants at night as it is difficult to identify them in the dark. Either bring along a flashlight or locate your plants during the day and mark them. Then, return at night to do your gathering.

Wearing a white, linen robe or spotlessly clean cloth clothes, take your tools and go to the spot. Remove all watches, gloves, shoes, and socks before actually approaching the herbs themselves.

In your strong hand, carry your magic knife, and in the other, the bag and bread. Walk to the herbs. With the tip of your knife, draw a circle clockwise in the earth around the plant.

Now standing, touch the blade of the magic knife to the herb and recite such words as these:

Thou has grown by favor of
the Sun, the Moon, and of the dew.
I make this intercession, ye herb:
I beseech thee to be of benefit

to me and my art,
for thy virtues are unfailing.
Thou art the dew of all the gods,
the eye of the Sun,
the light of the Moon,
the beauty and glory of the sky,
the mystery of the earth.
I purify thee so that whatsoever
is wrought by me with thee may,
in all its powers,
have a good and speedy effect with good success.
Be purified by my prayer and be powerful.

(Remember, recite this incantation slowly, with emphasis, as you stand touching the herb with your magic knife.)

When finished, gently cut a few sprigs, a few branches, or whatever amount you need. Never cut more than 25 percent of the growth (or growth from a very young plant) or the plant might not recover. As you cut, recite a little rune or simple phrase stating, in plain words, the reason why you need some of the herb. For instance, if you are cutting a cluster of yarrow flowers for a love spell, recite a love poem or a little rune such as the following:

I cut thee, yarrow,
so that love may grow.

After removing the leaves or stalks, bury a small piece of the bread near the base of the plant. This is in payment to the Earth for the part taken.

If removing the root (during the Waning Moon) dig up the earth surrounding the plant with the magic knife. This may take some time. When the root is visible and sufficiently clear, grasp the branches near the base of the plant and pull firmly, shaking it slightly if necessary to free it from the earth. It is best to fill the hole left by the root with red wine, a piece of bread, a few pennies, a bit of dried corn, and a small amount of honey, all of which can be mixed together at home and carried with you in a jar. Cover these treasures over with the removed dirt and return the spot to a natural-looking state.

Be sure that all cuttings and roots are placed in the cloth bag. They must not be allowed to touch the earth once they have been removed. They should also never be allowed to come into contact with iron, for iron destroys all magic.

Do not bother picking up leaves, blossoms, or seeds that lie on the ground; these are useless in magic, and should be left to produce more plants in the future.

When finished, take the herbs back home and prepare them for use.

Drying

Some herbs, such as borage, endive, snapdragon, and so on, are only used when fresh. Many others, however, can be dried and kept until needed. Here are procedures for drying herbs.

Discard all brown or insect-eaten leaves. Wash all cuttings or roots with pure water. Pat dry with a cloth or paper towel, making sure all mud, dirt, and other contaminants are removed.

To dry leaves, place the stalks on beds of paper towels spread on baking sheets. Turn them each day, making sure no mold begins to grow on them. Never allow them to lie in direct sunlight, or near an open window. In fact, the best room to dry your herbs is in a not-too-frequented room with good ventilation that is kept warm, either by the Sun or artificial means such as a fireplace, chimney (on second story), stove, etc.

(Ecologically-minded individuals are reminded that the paper towels can be used for clean-up jobs around the house after the herbs are dry.)

The leaves will be dry when they are crumbly or even crisp. Strip them off the stems and pick out the larger stems and woody matter.

To dry seeds and seed heads, such as the dill, anise, or coriander, gently tie together the stem ends and carefully place them in a paper sack. Tie the open end around the stem ends. The seed heads will be suspended within the bag so that no seeds will be lost during the drying process. These bags may be kept in full sunlight, or near the chimney. They dry quickly. Shake or roll the heads between your fingers to remove the seeds.

Pick out and discard the stems.

To dry flowers, such as roses, marigolds, lavender, yarrow, and so on, set on paper towels after washing and dry, as for leaves. Rose petals are best separated from the bed before drying. (Dry rose buds whole.) Lavender flowers and marigold are stripped from the stalk after drying, while the yarrow heads are sometimes left intact.

Roots dry very slowly; some say at least two years before they are completely dry! Hang them next to the chimney, or near the fire, or in any very warm spot.

The drying times of each herb varies, according to its sappiness and thickness. The most important factor to keep in mind is that the herbs must be absolutely dry, or mold will form in the storage jars and destroy the herb's usefulness.

If you need dried herbs in a hurry, hold them over an open fire, near the flames, as the old Witches used to do. Or, spread them on baking sheets and place them in a slow oven (about 200 degrees) for a few minutes. Watch them to make sure that they do not burst into flames, or turn brown.

Storing

Get a large quantity of bottles, dark-glassed ones being the best. Make sure that each is equipped with an air-tight stopper, cork, or lid. Have a good range of sizes. Wash and dry well. (Many magical herbalists load their dishwashers with the jars and let them run through the "sanitize" cycle, or through the whole cycle without adding any soap.)

Now make up a list of the herbs that you have to store (both those you have collected yourself and those store-bought). These will become labels. Beside each herb record the date picked (or bought), location grown (if known), and any other information you deem important. Cut these labels out.

As you gently fill each jar, paste on the appropriate label. Cork or screw on the lid, making sure that the seal is tight.

Ideally, herbs are kept in a specially constructed herb cabinet with sufficient space to allow some separation by planetary ruler, basic uses, etc. Realistically, this is not always possible. The important considerations are: be sure the herbs are out of direct sunlight, that the room has some air circulation, and that the cabinet, if possible, is made of wood without nails or metals of any kind.

Herbs cannot last forever, even dried herbs. New supplies should be obtained every seven months or so, or as stock dwindles. The store-bought herbs might be replaced sooner, since you can never be too sure how long they sat on the shelves in the store.

When herbs have lost their energies and new supplies have been obtained, return them to the earth and work them into the soil. This way they can become once again a part of the earth.

Above all, keep your herb cabinet clean, orderly, and up to date. It is the powerhouse of your magic, and so deserves special attention.

4

The Language of Magical Herbalism

Adept: One who is skilled in the art of magic.

Amulet: An object worn or carried to bring luck or to attract certain vibrations or people.

Anaphrodisiac: An herb that cools the passions.

Aphrodisiac: An herb that acts as a sexual excitant.

Athame: The sacred knife of the Witch, black-handled and often engraved with magic symbols.

Balefire: An open-air fire, a bonfire lit for magical purposes.

Bane: That which destroys life. Henbane, hellebore, and other such herbs are considered to be baneful.

Banish: To drive away an influence by magical means.

Besom: An old word meaning "broom." The Witch's broom is often called a besom.

Botanomancy: Divining the future through the use of herbs.

Censer: A vessel of brass, copper, clay, etc., in which incense is burned. Any object that is used in this manner.

Chaplet: A garland of flowers, leaves, or herbs worn on the head, as in the chaplets of laurel leaves worn by the classical Greeks and Romans as a symbol of honor.

Charge: To infuse with magical power or a specific magic purpose.

Charm: A spell or incantation.

Charm bag: A magical sachet.

Clairvoyance: Literally, "clear seeing." This is the ability to perceive facts, events, and other data by other than the five "normal" senses. Often referred to as intuition.

Clear: To drive out evil and negativity, especially from a place.

Consecrate: To make pure, holy, or sacred.

Coven: A group of Witches who meet to work magic and worship together.

Curse: A concentration of negative and destructive vibrations, deliberately formed and directed to a person, place, or thing.

Daphnomancy: Divining the future through the use of laurel leaves, usually by burning them and observing the smoke.

Deosil: Sunwise, clockwise. The direction in which all positive and beneficial actions are done in magic.

Divination: The art of finding things out by other than "normal" means, i.e., by magic.

Enchant: "Sing to." Magically speaking, a declaration of magical intent.

Exorcism: The act of casting out negative entities and general psychic clutter, usually from a place or object; rarely from a person.

Evil eye: Supposed glance capable of causing great harm or ill luck.

Fluid condenser: A substance that concentrates and stores natural energies, or "fluids." In herbal magic, liquid fluid condensers are often used to concentrate the power of a specific herb for magical use.

Grimoire: A collection of spells and magical rituals.

Handfasting: A Witch wedding ceremony. More broadly, all weddings and solemn betrothals.

Hallucinogen: An herb that causes perception of objects or events with no basis in reality, a mind-altering substance. Hallucinogen-induced "visions" are not manifestations of true clairvoyance; they are purely mental recreation.

Herb: Any plant used in magic.

Herbal: A collection of information regarding the properties, use, and symbolism of herbs.

Hex: Popularly believed to be an evil spell. It is derived from the German word for Witch.

Incantation: A chant spoken with fierce conviction, often using repetition, rhyme, or heavy emphasis of certain words.

Infusion: An herbal potion or tea. To make an infusion, steep one-half ounce dried herb to one pint water.

Invocation: A prayer or plea to a higher being, usually a god or goddess.

Leech: An old Anglo-Saxon word for "healer." Leeches employed herbs and magic in their work, known as "leechcraft" or "leechdom."

Macerate: To soak in alcohol or oil.

Magic: The manipulation of psychic forces to cause change. Within the boundaries of this work, magic is the art of tapping the hidden powers of herbs and plants and using them to produce changes in our own lives and those of our friends and loved ones.

Magician: A person of either sex who practices magic.

Magus: A male magician.

Narcotic: A sleep- or coma-producing substance.

Pentagram: A five-pointed star, such as the one used in the blessing of the Magic Garden. Some times erroneously referred to as a "pentacle." The latter is, strictly speaking, an object upon which a pentagram or other magical symbols are painted, engraved, or carved. The pentagram is an ancient symbol of protection.

Poppet: A small image of a human being or animal then handled in ritual to influence a specific person or animal. The destructive "voodoo doll" is a popularized vulgarization of the poppet. Among Witches, the poppet is generally used to effect healing. The doll is also called a "fith-fath."

Rede: A maxim, tenet, or rule of life. An unwritten law, often in rhyme.

Runes: 1) Short, rhymed chants. 2) Ancient magical symbols. 3) A magical alphabet.

Sabbat: One of the eight religious festivals of Witches. They occur on the solstices and equinoxes and also on October 31 (Samhain or Hallows), February 2 (Lupercalia or Candlemas), April 30 (Beltane or Roodmas), and August 1 (Lughnasad or Lammas).

Sachet: A small, cloth bag stuffed with herbs.

Scry: To gaze into a crystal ball, fire, pool of ink, etc., to awaken and summon clairvoyant powers.

Simple: A one-herb potion or infusion. A "compound" is an infusion of several herbs.

Spell: A magical ritual performed to cause change.

Steep: To soak in a hot liquid, such as water.

Three-fold Law: The Witch's rede that states whatever one does returns to them three-fold, "three times ill or three times good," and thus encourages us to "harm none," another Witch's rede.

Tincture: An infusion made in alcohol or apple cider vinegar.

Tisane: A French term for an herbal tea.

Wicca: An old name for Witchcraft.

Widdershins: Counterclockwise, the direction of negativity.

Wise woman or cunning man: The village herbalist who worked magic and often acted as doctor, confessor, midwife, psychologist, and priest(ess).

Witch: A male or female follower of the Witchcraft religion.

Witchcraft: The ancient religion based on the worship of the lifeforce of the universe, as personified by a god and goddess. Its beliefs include reincarnation and the three-fold law. Most Witches practice magic.

Wort: An old word meaning "herb." Mugwort, St. John's wort, etc., preserve the word.

Wortcunning: The use of herbs, usually in magic.

Yarb: A dialectical form of the word "herb."

PART TWO

Herbal Secrets

5

Protection

Of all the powers that herbs possess, perhaps the most widely used are those that are protective. These are the herbs that disperse evil and set up a powerful protective barrier wherever they are burned, hung up, or carried.

Since these herbs are possessed of good or positive vibrations, they automatically work to repel negative, or *evil,* vibrations. Thus, when these negative vibes come up against a psychic energy barrier of positive vibrations, the negativity is bounced back. Protection is conferred.

All operations of protection are best done in the Waxing Moon. Red and white are the colors most commonly used for sachets, altar decorations, flowers, etc. Place a white cloth on the altar. On it arrange white, brand-new candles in candle holders and a vase of protective flowers, such as snapdragons, cyclamen, or rue blossoms, and some greens like trefoil, juniper, or rosemary.

For your ritual bath, add a few grains dragon's blood bath salts, if available, or make up your own protective bath salts by putting one cup sea salt into a jar, and adding several drops rosemary, frankincense, or any other protective oil. Keep adding and mixing until all particles are moistened. Let sit for several days. Store in a dark, cool place.

To use, add three pinches to a very warm (or, if you feel up to it, very cold) tubful of water. After drying, anoint yourself with a protective oil, such as rosemary, rose geranium, hyssop, basil, or frankincense.

Burn pure frankincense or myrrh in your censer for a powerful incense, or use the following blend in equal parts: frankincense, wood betony, and dragon's blood. Then, while the smoke seethes and swirls around you, do your protective magic! (There are varieties of dragon's blood that are harmful. Some can cause pregnant women to abort. Be cautious.)

Protective Herbs

The list of herbs possessing protective properties is quite lengthy, but the most-often used are mentioned here.

Angelica	Cyclamen
Asafoetida	Dill
Ash twigs and leaves	Elderberries or leaves
Avens	Fennel
Balm of Gilead	Fern
Basil	Flax
Bay laurel	Fumitory
Betony	Horehound

Hyssop	Rosemary
Juniper	Rowan
Mistletoe	Rue
Mugwort	St. John's wort
Mullein	Snapdragon
Peony roots	Tarragon
Periwinkle	Trefoil
Pimpernel	Vervain
Rose geranium	

Use this list when making up sachets and protective amulets. (*Note:* Angelica closely resembles poisonous hemlock, which can be fatal. Take care to identify it correctly.)

Protection Sachets and Other Protective Charms

One of the most effective protective charms is the protection sachet.

Get a piece of white cotton cloth, seven inches square. Next, select three, seven, or nine of the dried herbs listed above. Take equal parts of each and place them into an earthenware bowl. Mix them together silently for a few moments with your hands and then set aside.

Spread out the cloth on your altar. Transfer the herbs to the center of the cloth. Gather up the corners and, with a red piece of string, yarn, or thread, tie firmly around the gathered-up corners, capturing the herbs inside. As you tie the first knot, say in a firm voice:

I bind thee to protect this house and all within it.

Knot twelve times more, repeating the above with each repetition. When finished, stand, facing north, holding aloft your magic knife in your strong hand, the sachet in the other. With the tip of the knife pressed against the sachet, say such words as these:

May this that I have fashioned tonight
serve as guardian and protection for this house
and all who reside within it.
May it serve me well.

If the sachet is being made for a car, boat, or other vehicle, substitute the proper words.

Now, hang it up by its red thread, in the highest point in the house. If this is impossible, hang it inside a closet, or over the main entrance.

When used in cars or other vehicles, place it under the driver's seat. It is also good to make up a few extras to hang over the doorstep, or to bury in the garden. They are truly all-purpose protective devices.

A simpler method of making an herbal protective was used extensively not more than one hundred years ago in the British Isles and on the Continent. Pick several protective herbs and bind the stems together with red thread, then hang up. This practice dates back to Babylonian times.

A close cousin to this was very popular in Italy a few centuries ago and is still effective. Get a twig of rowan on May Day (for best results). Twine several dozen yards of red thread or yarn around it, then place it in a window where it will be visible. This is an all-purpose protective charm.

At one time, Witches hung an acorn in every room in the window to protect the house. Some put a whole mandrake on the hearth for similar reasons.

Anti-lightning charms, for those who live in lightning-prone places, can be made of mistletoe, hawthorn, and bay laurel. Tie up as with the protection sachet, but use silver or white thread. Hang up in the chimney, or on the chimney, or in the highest point of the house.

Garlic, one of the most powerful of all protective herbs, was once placed beneath the pillows of sleeping children to protect them at night. A string of garlic helps ward off diseases, but do not hang it around your neck. Hang it up in the bedroom.

Onions are very protective. A half-onion is kept in the kitchen to absorb diseases and ill luck. It should be replaced every few days.

Babies are given necklaces of cloves that are hung in cribs or in the cradle as a safeguard against diseases and other ills, but be sure to keep all plants out of baby's reach.

Finally, for a personal protective charm, take twigs from an oak or rowan tree. Put them down on your altar into a solar cross shape (equal-armed cross, the antecedent of the Christian symbol). Bind them together in this shape with red thread. Touch it with the point of your magic knife and infuse it with protective purpose, saying these or similar words:

Rowan (or oaken) tree and scarlet thread,
I conjure thee to be a protection
and safeguard against all adversity and evil.
Protect me well.

Always wear or carry it with you (it can be placed in your wallet, purse, etc.). The same charm can be made of larger branches and hung up in a room for protection.

As with all things, prevention is easier than curing. When protective measures have not been taken, or maintained, however, purifications are sometimes necessary.

Purifications

Purification is the casting out of negativity, evil influences, etc. It is usually performed when a sense of tension or uneasiness is felt in a house, particularly if several people notice it.

It is always performed just prior to moving into a new home or apartment, to be sure that no vibrations are left behind from the last tenants.

Then again, some magicians perform a purification ceremony every three months to keep the home harmonious and pleasant.

The best time to perform purification ceremonies is during the Waning Moon. A purification is a minor form of exorcism. Be absolutely certain that you are alone in the house or apartment. After your bath and anointing, you will dress in a white robe or clothes (you'll be leaving the house halfway through the ritual, so dress accordingly). Open all windows, cover all food, and remove all pets including cats, dogs, reptiles, birds, even fish. There are to be no living things in the house save yourself.

If you are doing the ritual at a friend's house, be sure that these preparations are carried out, and keep your friend out of the house. Take your bath and do your anointing directly before going to the house that needs purification, if it is not your own home.

Light the twin candles on the white altar cloth and set a quantity of the following incense alight in the censer (again, if at someone else's home, set up a small altar there):

Purification incense: Bay, avens, mugwort, yarrow, rosemary, St. John's wort, angelica, basil, juniper berries—equal parts of each. Powder and mix in the mortar and pestle.

While the incense is smoking in the censer, take several garlic cloves, one for each room of the house (including attics, garages, basements, etc.). Peel the outer skin off the garlic and place one in each room, in the center of the floor. If you have very bad feelings about one room in particular place one peeled clove garlic in each corner of that room.

Now, add more incense to the censer and carry it with you, going from room to room in the house, thoroughly censing the area. If you have a swinging censer, swing the bowl in a counterclockwise direction, which is the direction of banishing, of clearing. Clockwise is the direction of invocation.

When finished (do not forget attics, etc.), add more incense to the censer and place it, on a length of aluminum foil, in the center of the house on the floor. Leave the building (stand outside, sit on the front porch, in the car, whatever) for about thirteen minutes. (Wait until you feel that it is time to go back in).

Once back inside, gather up the garlic cloves, without touching them, put them in a plastic bag and put in the trash. Leave the candles burning for the rest of the evening. You can burn a little frankincense to purify the atmosphere. But the purification incense should never be burned while people are in the house.

Protection Wreath

As a closing to this chapter, the construction of the charming protection wreath is quite fitting.

Take several long branches of fresh rosemary, from one to two feet long. Fashion them into a circular shape, tying the ends together with fine green cotton thread. When the basic wreath shape has been accomplished, flesh it out with additional rosemary, securely tying the individual sprigs to the main body of the wreath.

When the wreath is full enough for your tastes, tie a red ribbon into a bow at the top or bottom of the wreath. Next, pluck any of these protective herbs from the garden or wilds and insert them into the twined rosemary: bay laurel, vervain, mistletoe, rue, mugwort, hyssop, fennel, basil, etc. The dried seed heads of rue, dill, and fennel work well too. Make sure the wreath has a well-balanced appearance, and that all herbs are firmly attached to the rosemary.

Now, collect several of these flowers and poke three, seven, or nine into the wreath for added protection: snapdragons, cyclamen, garlic flowers, marigolds, carnations, or roses. Attach string or a fine steel wire to the wreath in two places and hang up wherever protection is needed: over the hearth, on the front door, or in windows.

Any protective herbs may be used in this powerful wreath. The fresh flowers will have to be replaced at regular intervals but the herbs will dry beautifully.

6

Divination

For centuries, Witches have been renowned for their ability to see into the future. They do this through two different means: divination and clairvoyance.

Divination is the art of finding things out through the use of other than normal means. Crystal balls, dowsing rods, pendulums, the tarot, the I Ching, and other tools used in divination.

Clairvoyance is the capability to *see clearly,* to be consciously psychic and to be able to attain this state without the use of aids (such as those listed above). Clairvoyants or psychics who can be consciously clairvoyant do not need to use divination. For those who cannot tap their psychic powers, divination serves as a means of awakening *the sight,* as it is also known.

Some methods of divination enable the practitioner to focus the mind so that clairvoyance can be coaxed to the surface. Others simply hone psychic powers to a fine point.

Still other methods of divination do not call on clairvoyance at all, but work through totally different means.

Those who are clairvoyant do not need divination; those who are not, do. Everyone is born psychic, but during early childhood training we learn to suppress this talent, and it is only when an interest is taken in the subject that most of us relearn its use. Fortunately, herbs can help in lifting the veil that separates tomorrow from today.

There are no hard and fast rules about divinatory rituals. Many herbs work best while the user is asleep, with the answers to your questions coming in the form of dreams. Some help promote a restful meditation, which stills the conscious mind to the point that psychic messages may become known.

There is no basic altar setup for these rituals. Yellow candles are sometimes burned, but white work just as well.

Add a bit of anise oil to the bath water to attune yourself psychically before divining. A little nutmeg oil rubbed on the forehead helps the clairvoyant powers.

If you wish to anoint yourself with a special oil, blend equal parts of anise, acacia, and cassia oils and use this Witches' sight oil.

Divination Incenses

Following are a few much-favored incense recipes that permeate the atmosphere with ideal vibrations for divinatory practices.

It is important to remember the difference between true clairvoyance and drug-induced visions. Hallucinogenic herbs were once used to produce visions but the Witch of today rarely resorts to such practices. Most of the prophecies made while under the influence of such incenses were pure fantasy.

Witches' sight incense: This is an all-purpose formula, to be burned while reading tarot cards, using crystals, meditating, etc. It is composed of gum mastic, patchouli, cinnamon, juniper, and sandalwood.

On a Wednesday, during the Waxing Moon, take equal parts of the powdered herbs, mix well, and moisten with a few drops of mingled musk and ambergris oils. (The artificial ambergris will work; ambrette oil will do for the musk. If these are unavailable, use clove and nutmeg.)

Mix until all particles are moistened, crumbly but not soggy. Let stand overnight, then pack in a jar, leaving the cork slightly loose.

Scrying incense: Many Witches employ crystal balls in their divination sessions. To strengthen the crystal, rub it with fresh mugwort leaves. While scrying (gazing), burn an incense composed of mugwort and wormwood, equal parts. Place the ball on the altar between two white candles, with the censer back on the other side of the ball.

Vision incense: To be burned when no props, such as cards, are to be used. Contacts the subconscious mind and allows that which is unknown to become known:

3 parts cinquefoil

3 parts chicory root

1 part clove

Grind together on a Wednesday night.

In all acts of divination, the mind must be stilled and quiet. All outside noises and concerns must be shut out and the mind must be at rest. Clear it of everyday cares and problems.

If there is a specific question you wish answered, keep this in mind as you perform any of the following procedures. If not, keep the mind open and be prepared to receive any information forthcoming. Though you may not at first understand the message or information, all will become clear with time.

Clairvoyance Brews

The cauldron, traditional tool of the Witch, was often employed in the preparation of a *clairvoyance brew.* The Witch filled the cauldron with spring water and then hung it over a fire on a tripod. When the water was boiling, she threw into the pot shredded bay laurel leaves, mugwort, and cinquefoil. The Witch then manipulated the lid to direct and concentrate the steam rising from the bubbling cauldron. Inhaling it, she entered a psychic state and called out predictions to her clients.

The same method can be used on your gas flame. Take your pot (the one reserved for herbal magic) and fill it half-full with bottled or fresh spring water. Let it sit over the flame until bubbling. Add the above herbs to the water and cover tightly. Take off the flame and move to the altar, setting the pot on a hot pad (preferably one made of wood). The candles should already be lit.

Using a potholder, if necessary, lift the lid and inhale the vapors deeply several times. Do this for a few minutes, alternating between steam and air.

(In magic, better results will be obtained by using the diaphragm while breathing. To find your diaphragm, touch yourself just above the navel, below and between the ribcages. As you breathe in, push this area out with your breath. This is natural breathing, very useful in magical operations.)

You should feel calm, relaxed, peaceful, and slightly drowsy. Any of the various methods of divination may be readily practiced now.

If you wish to make direct contact with your subconscious mind (the source of your psychic messages, the clairvoyant part of your mind), still all thoughts and sit quietly after inhaling the steam.

Note any pictures and symbols that come to your mind. If they are richly detailed pictures, far outside your usual range of thoughts, note them carefully. These are the things that visions are made of. Afterward, write down everything, for future reference.

Another way to use the clairvoyance brew is to inhale it just before going to bed. Your dreams may become prophetic and revealing.

Herb Scrying

Get a small quantity of dried patchouli, mugwort, or wormwood. Crumble the herb between your hands until it is finely diminished.

Next, pour it into a small square pan (glass or ceramic). Light yellow candles and place the pan on your working area. Close your eyes, extend the index finger of your weak hand, and gently touch the center of the pan with its tip.

Move it at random in the pan, shifting from one direction to another without conscious pattern. Keep this up for a few minutes.

Now, remove your finger, open your eyes, and interpret the symbols you have just written in the herb. If desired, scrying incense can be burned during this rite. It may be repeated several times.

Simples

A *simple* is an infusion of a single herb. To make a clairvoyance simple, boil one pint water in your pot. In a teapot put one-half ounce mugwort, thyme, rosemary, or yarrow in a cup and pour the water over it. Let steep for ten minutes, then strain, using a bamboo or other nonmetallic strainer. Sweeten with a little honey if desired, clover and orange being traditional. (Yarrow in large or frequent doses taken over a long period of time may be potentially harmful. Yarrow contains thyjone, considered toxic.)

These teas are useful in developing the clairvoyant powers especially if drunk every time one attempts to achieve clairvoyance.

They are especially soothing and effective if sipped while in the ritual bath.

Listening to the Wind

This is one of the old charges brought against Witches during the Persecution. Actually it is one of the most pleasant, easy, and effective modes of divination.

On a windy day, just before dusk or quite early in the morning, lie down among tall, leafy trees, far from roadways and other noisy places.

Close your eyes and relax, feeling the earth supporting your body. Listen to the gentle breeze's melody as it moves through the leaves above you. Listen long enough and you may begin to hear voices in the winds.

These are the whispers of the wind. They cannot be captured on recording tape, or proved by scientists to be anything other than creations of your own mind.

But the Witches know that such whispers, induced by the hypnotic voice of the wind, are actually messages from beyond the conscious mind and often carry important messages.

Herbal Pendulums

The use of pendulums is widespread. A heavy object is attached to a string and answers to questions are interpreted by its movements.

To make an herbal pendulum, take an herb such as orris root, a lump of frankincense, a star anise seed, a chip of sandalwood, or a piece of cinnamon bark. Get a natural fiber thread of a light yellow color and firmly tie this around the herb, making sure that the knot will not slip (you can drill a hole through the herb and pass the thread through it).

Now, measure off the thread, the width of your out-stretched little finger to thumb, and then the width of the widest part of your hand. Cut it so that this length remains. Hold the end between the thumb and forefinger of your strong hand, resting the elbow on the table. Now ask a yes-no question, one you need an answer for.

The pendulum will start to move, either in a circular motion or back and forth. The circular motion usually signifies yes, while the back and forth signifies no. If it does not move at all there is no answer, or you are not to know the answer, or you already know the answer, and have no reason to be asking the question in the first place! This is one of the many ways to tap the subconscious mind.

Sachets and Pillows

Inhaling the scents of dried and fresh herbs can produce clairvoyant states, often operating best while asleep.

Find a small pillow case, about nine by nine inches. or sew one yourself. Stuff with about one-quarter pound dried mugwort (more or less to fill it). Now, sew up the open end. Place it on top of your regular pillow and sleep on it.

The mugwort pillow induces clairvoyant dreams. Sleep on it for several nights in a row.

A good, all-purpose dream pillow very popular one hundred years or so ago can be mixed of equal parts of lemon balm, costmary, rose petals, mint, and cloves. Construct and use as the mugwort pillow.

Frankincense and Laurel

Both of these herbs have a long history in divining the future. Light several charcoal blocks in the censer and let sit until glowing. Throw on a few laurel leaves, fresh if you can get them. Ask a question while doing this. If the leaves make loud sounds and burn brightly, it will be a favorable time, or the answer is yes. If they sputter and die out, it is unfavorable, or the answer is no.

If you have a fireplace, throw a handful of powdered frankincense onto the fire. If the flames rise up in one mass, it is a good sign. If they are divided a little, unfortunate. If they rise in three points, a great event will happen soon. If they are much dispersed it is not a good sign. Crackling and snapping fortell misfortune, and if the whole fire is suddenly extinguished by the frankincense when it is thrown on or soon thereafter, great danger is eminent.

Another method uses poppy seeds, the black variety. When scattered on coals, if the smoke rises lightly and disappears quickly it is a good sign. But if the smoke hangs heavy and low, the opposite is true.

These methods of divination have been used by Witches since the days of classical Rome, usually to determine the condition of a loved one far from home.

The procedures and rituals outlined in this chapter are based upon the occult principle that all humans are born with psychic powers. These are lying latent within most of us. Herbs, fortunately, are there to help us strengthen and nurture these powers.

7

Healing

Many Witches combine their magical knowledge of herbs with the medicinal side as well, finding that the two often work in tandem for added power. Herbal cures are frequently boosted with a dash of magic to speed the healing process.

Though this book is not concerned with the medicinal value of herbs, a chapter on the magical use of herbs in healing is well within our major subject. Discussed in this chapter are the herbs used to magically cure, help speed recovery, and to prevent one from getting sick in the first place.

The basis of magical healing is just that, magic. It uses the powers of the herbs fortified and directed by the healer to heal the body directly through the force of magic.

Though the Witches have complicated magical procedures of healing, sometimes using poppets or stand-ins to represent the sick individual, there are other methods of healing, those involving herbs, which can be used by anyone, Witch or non-Witch.

One word of warning: magic is not to be used in the place of professional medical attention. For serious injuries or illnesses, consult a physician as any non-Witch or Witch would do. These remedies are mainly used for lesser maladies. such as headaches, colds, warts, and so on.

It must be repeated that most herbal magic is not instantaneous. For some afflictions, some time must pass before complete results will be obtained. During this time the ritual should be repeated.

For those interested in the medicinal properties of herbs, consult the books listed in the bibliography. If this is the course you wish to take, do remember to follow instructions carefully, as herbs are quite potent and many are poisonous taken in unusually large amounts. And remember, it never hurts to add a little incantation of power over any simple or poultice you make up!

The ancients believed that illnesses were created by evil spirits that inhabited the bodies of the sick. Once the spirits were exorcised, the person got well. Witches feel that illnesses are caused by strains put upon the body by imbalance. Overindulgence in smoking, alcohol, drugs, sex, or work, as well as neglect of the need for physical activity, leave gaps in the body's natural defenses both spiritual and physical.

When the body is weakened, illnesses find easy access and begin to do their dirty work. Viruses and communicable diseases are around us at all times, so it is easy to see how important it is to keep our lives balanced and, therefore, healthy.

Organic diseases, such as cancer, are usually self-induced. Drugs. tobacco, and poor eating habits are the main culprits.

The processed, chemically pumped foods that we daily consume are also battering away at our defense systems, the chemicals combining in our bodies with unknown and potentially dangerous results.

By banishing cigarettes, alcohol, drugs, refined sugar, bleached flour, fat-soaked and artificially preserved and flavored foods, many diseases can be prevented before they need to be cured.

But when disease or simple complaints occur, many turn to herbs to relieve the pain and cure the patient.

For the more major diseases, full-blown magical rituals are often required. They are conducted by a whole coven (group) of Witches. In this work, true miracles are often performed: tumors can be dissolved, cancer eliminated, and cells regrown. The simple use of herbs in magic are overshadowed by such feats. It might be wise, however, to check with the herbalists, for many are claiming great success through long-term herbal treatments of even the most deadly and stubborn illnesses.

There are, fortunately, many do-it-yourself spells and rituals designed to give comfort during a time of sickness, or to relieve another's pain. The road back to health must not only be paved with a positive-thinking mind, but also with such herbal spells and procedures as will help.

Attitude is of the utmost importance. When preparing charms for yourself or for others, keep in your mind a vision of the person completely whole, healed, and free of disease, injury, or whatever is the current problem.

Negative thinking has no place in magic, so do not dwell on the illness or injury; forget it and concentrate on health and happiness.

When first beginning to work on an illness, determine the exact nature of the trouble. You can do this through clairvoyance, or with the aid of medical advice perhaps already offered. Of course, if the malady is easily identified, then there will be no problem.

Next, look to the Moon. Illnesses, warts, and pimples are banished during the Waning Moon. Rituals during the Waxing Moon are recommended for speedy healing of injuries and wounds.

Whether or not the person is present, always let them know of your actions. If this is impossible (i.e., they are far away, or unconscious, or if you cannot contact them for any other reason) meditate for a few minutes before beginning to make certain that your efforts will not be wasted. A person who does not wish to be healed rarely receives any benefits from magic, for their negative thinking blocks all but the most powerful magic.

(It is not necessary or even helpful to have the sufferer present. If they are, have them sit in your magic room, but out of your sight while you perform the magic.)

Drape your altar with blue cloth and have blue candles on it for your rite of healing. After your bath, anoint your forehead, neck, hands, wrists, and soles of the feet with healing oil.

Healing oil: Gather together equal parts sandalwood chips, fresh red carnation petals, and rosemary leaves. Crush slightly and then pack them into a green-glassed jar. Pour purified olive oil over them and cap tightly. Let sit for seven days where it will receive the Sun's rays during the day and the Moon's rays at night. Afterward, strain and store in the green-glass jar.

This oil may be kept for long periods ready to be used as needed. To help preserve it, add a few drops of benzoin tincture (see chapter 9).

Healing incense and saffron water: In the censer, burn a healing incense, such as one composed of myrrh, rose buds, and saffron ground together. Have a bowl of saffron water on the altar as well. To make saffron water, boil one pint spring water. Add one table-spoon saffron. Cover with a cloth and let sit three minutes. Then strain the water through the cloth into a blue or crystal-clear bowl. Set on the southern point of the altar.

Wash your hands in the saffron water before actu-ally beginning the rite, then dry your hands on a small cloth placed nearby for this purpose. Next, say a heal-ing invocation to the deity you invoke. A Witch who worships Isis might use something like the following:

Isis,
you who are all that ever was,
all that is,
and all that shall be,
heal me as you healed Horus of all his wounds
which Set, his brother, had inflicted on him.
O Isis,

great magician,
heal me,
and deliver me
from all fatal sicknesses,
wounds,
and evil things,
and from diseases of every kind.

Naturally, if using this invocation for another person, you would insert his or her name into the text, in place of *me*. Next, use any of the following rituals.

Healing Amulets

A good all-purpose amulet is fashioned from one peeled clove of garlic, a pinch of eucalyptus, a pinch of cinnamon, two pinches of sage, and one pinch saffron. Sew up in a blue cloth and anoint with sandalwood oil. This is to be carried at all times by the afflicted until the problem is gone.

For lung complaints, try using spearmint in the heating amulet along with the rest of the herbs. For problems with the head or mind, add a little rosemary. Eye complaints indicate eyebright or camomile. For any other illnesses, the basic amulet will be fine.

Other very beneficial healing oils to wear or to anoint the sufferer with are carnation (do not use for burns), lavender, lotus, narcissus, sandalwood, violet, rosemary, and myrrh. Rue oil is sometimes used, but can set up severe allergic reactions in some people, so it should be used only when nothing else is available.

Remember while sewing up the sachet to concentrate on healing vibrations. You should already be infused with these energies for the healing oil attunes the body to this plane.

When the amulet is finished, wrap it up in a green cloth and give it to the patient, hang it around the neck if it is for you, or store in a safe place until it can be delivered.

Every three days until the illness is gone, anoint with sandalwood oil. If the person will be far away, say a healing rune over a bottle of the oil and give it to them, with strict instructions.

Healing Wounds

For injuries and wounds, a different form of magic is often used. This is sometimes called *assumption of the oak*. In this, a dressing that has been used on the wound is sprinkled with rue oil and hidden inside a hole hollowed in an oak tree. A natural hollow works best. This is done during the Waning Moon, for the wound is being banished from the person and being transferred to the tree, from which it will be dispersed into the earth.

Anoint the injured person with carnation oil to speed healing and regrowth of the damaged area of his or her body.

Wart Cures

To remove warts, pimples, blemishes, and other like growths, a banishing ritual is often used. Take a small dried bean and rub it against the imperfections. Dig a hole in the ground and drop the bean into it, saying something like, "As this bean decays so my wart will go away" (or pimple, etc.). This, like all banishing rituals, should be performed during the Waning Moon. Use a different bean for every blemish.

Onions and Garlic

The onion is one of the earliest and most widely used antisickness amulets. They are used to absorb diseases so that they will not spread throughout the household. Not more than one hundred years ago, it was quite common for the cook to keep a half-onion under the sink to keep disease from starting in the kitchen.

Onions are rubbed on the soles of the feet or the afflicted part of the body to absorb the disease, in certain parts of the world. The onion is then discarded.

Still another old magical cure-all is garlic. Nearly everybody knows it as the traditional charm to ward off vampires, but few are aware that a necklace made of garlic flowers or even the bulbs themselves also drives away illness.

Garlic is often used in place of the onion in magic. Both herbs are attributed to Mars, the planet of war, and both wage battles on illnesses of every kind.

To aid the sufferer to regain his or her health, put a vase of fresh wood sorrel in the sickroom, a wild herb that shoots up in the early months of spring. If these are not available, use thistles, which are excellent vitalizers and help the body to heal itself.

Headaches

This is one of the most frequent demons to plague us. Television, air pollution, and the horrendous noise of the city are all major contributors to the malady. Fortunately, the Witches have preserved numerous remedies, one of which is sure to cure all but the most stubborn ache.

The oldest cure is to gather any herb (usually ivy) growing on the head of a statue. Bind this loosely around the sufferer's head with a light-blue thread and it will lessen even violent pain.

A pillow sewn up of mugwort leaves also helps a headache, as will one of the fresh leaves stuck up the nose.

Another cure is to sew up into a small light-blue sachet equal parts of the following herbs: lavender, mandrake, peppermint, mugwort, clove, marjoram, and orange peel. Tie the sachet onto a blue thread or cord and wear around the neck to prevent headaches from occurring. Sniffing any of these herbs is also said to help.

Garlands are often featured in headache cures. Among these are garlands of violets or fresh pennyroyal worn on the head. (Ingesting the essential oil of pennyroyal can be lethal. Skin contact of the essential oil can also cause dermatitis.)

Two more cures: fresh bruised leaves of bergamot, mint, and lavender pressed on to the forehead should allay the pain, and the peel of the cucumber bound to the forehead cools the pain.

Colds

This is probably the second-most bothersome of modern illnesses. The most advanced medical research has not wiped out this common condition. Witches, however, have all the answers. The best thing to do is to prevent the cold from happening by the following method.

Quarter white onions and place one in every room of the house as a protection against colds. If one already has a cold, place garlic or onions in his or her room every day to keep the cold from spreading.

A good all-purpose cold herb is the eucalyptus. Sew up a sachet of this herb in a blue cloth and either wear or carry with you during the cold season. For those who live or travel in desert communities, especially cities like Las Vegas or Palm Springs, these charms are absolutely indispensable. Walking from air-conditioned cars to the hot desert air into chilly hotel lobbies is an excellent method of contracting colds.

Another good cure is the regular application of eucalyptus oil. Anoint the forehead, throat, and wrists.

Old Witches say that if one eats an onion everyday he or she will never catch a cold, never!

Animals

Finally, a curious remedy to cure an animal: if you have an animal with an open wound, gather four red thistle blossoms before the break of day, and put one in each of the four points of the compass with a stone in the middle. Upon this stone place the animal and have it stay there for several minutes.

The power of this spell is the thistle, which gives off tremendous vitalizing energy. The circle contains and directs the powers of the thistles, which are aligned with the four directions, and, so, the four elements. An animal sitting in the center of this arrangement (or a person, certainly) would receive a great deal of energy, excellent for strengthening their own healing powers to heal their wounds.

When you or your patient is healthy again, make up a little sachet of dried rue and wear it at all times to avert disease.

Above all, live a balanced, healthy, and happy life.

© Robin Wood 1986

8

Love

Love is the most magical, mystical, binding, destructive, and uplifting of all energies. It can transcend time and space, alter loyalties, even cause wars and revolutions.

There are herbs that vibrate on a *love* level. These are used to draw love to the bearer or user. Magicians and Witches never try to force anyone into love. Magic like that is evil, as it attempts to control another person.

The herbs of love vibrate on a friendly and attracting plane. They set up an aura around the user that is irresistibly interesting and compelling.

Most are sweetly scented, such as flowery and fruity scents, although perhaps every herb has been used at one time or another in the frantic search for love.

From the literally thousands of love spells and rituals designed to draw a love into one's life, there are a few presented here. It must be remembered that never is another human being to be trapped magically and pulled into a love affair. Serious consequences face the person who attempts this.

The love altar is laid out with pinks and whites. Lay a pink altar cloth out and use pink candles. Anoint the candles with a rose or apple-blossom oil prior to your ritual, or anoint with your favorite perfume or cologne. Place on the charcoal a love incense, such as the following.

Love Incense

On a Friday mix together lavender, dragon's blood, myrtle, rose petals, orris, and three drops each of musk and patchouli oils. Mix evenly and then spread out to dry on a nonmetallic surface where it can remain undisturbed for one week. On the next Friday crumble the incense and place it in a bottle with a fast-fitting stopper. Burn three spoonfuls as needed. (There are many varieties of dragon's blood. Be sure to research all of them. Some are harmful and can cause pregnant women to abort.)

Sachets

To attract a man, mix together lavender, dried bachelor's buttons, and a tiny pinch of valerian root. Add a bay leaf and carry with you wherever you go.

To attract a woman, use patchouli, cinnamon, and henbane. (The latter traditionally gathered by the man in the morning, while standing naked on one foot!) Or, carry a whole orris root in a green silk bag to attract lovers.

A good all-purpose love spell using a sachet can be performed as follows: take the petals of roses (well dried), a pinch of catnip, half a handful of yarrow, a touch of mint, coltsfoot, strawberry leaves, well-ground orris root, tansy, and a bit of vervain. Mix well on a Friday evening in the Moon's increase, and divide into three parts.

Take one of the parts, go outside naked, bend down on one knee, and throw the herbs up to the Moon, asking that love be sent to you.

Now go inside and scatter the second part around your bedroom. Sew the third and last part up in a green or pink cloth and wear this on your body, and love will surely appear.

Here is a list of the most useful sachet herbs to use in sachets and love rituals. With this list you can make up your own charms, sachets, and spells.

Do not compose anything edible from this list. Feeding someone a love potion is not in keeping with the *harm none* policy of magic. Besides, many of these ingredients are poisonous when taken internally.

Apple	Henbane
Aster	Jasmine
Bachelor's buttons	Lavender
Basil myrtle	Lemon balm
Bergamot	Lovage
Balm of Gilead	Mandrake
Caraway	Marjoram
Coriander	Meadowsweet
Cumin	Orris root
Dragon's blood	Periwinkle
Elecampane	Pink geranium

Rose	Tormentil
Rosemary	Vervain
Southernwood	Violet
Tonka beans	Yarrow

Subtle Sorcery

If your heart is set on one particular man or woman, present him or her with fresh flowers, such as jasmine, violets, red roses, pink geraniums, or asters. These flowers make clear your intent, for they vibrate on a very high love rate. Never send or give yellow or white roses to a lover or intended lover if at all possible.

Flowers in the language of magic symbolize sexuality as well as love.

If you wish to add some spice to your love affair, give your lover some carnations. The red blossoms have the greatest effect. Carnations are packed with energy and their spicy fragrance hints at exotic pleasures.

Marriage and Fertility Charms

Carry a sachet of orange flowers to get the word out that you are in the mood for marriage.

Carry a bagful of hazel nuts to ensure your own fertility, or give to a bride to ensure hers.

Other herbs to ensure fertility are basil, hazel, poppy, cucumber, apple, pomegranate, acorns, myrtle, and all nuts. Men should carry a piece of mandrake root to ensure their own fertility and sexual prowess, while the jasmine flower does the same for women. The first seven herbs listed above can be added to food and taken internally to ensure proper fertility, or they can be introduced into sachets, as can acorns, myrtle, and nuts.

Yarrow makes an excellent marriage charm. On a Friday during the Waxing Moon, take nine dried yarrow flower heads. Bind the stems together with a copper wire. Then, tie a small bow over the wire with a green ribbon. Present it to the married couple, with the instructions to hang it over their bed. Or place it on the headboard.

If you get into a fight with your husband or wife, wear the oil of basil and endeavor to have him or her smell it. Both tempers will instantly be soothed and calmed.

When Love Has Died

If your love leaves you, or if you have decided that it is time to get out, carry one of the following herbs, for they help mend a love-ravaged heart: balm of Gilead, valerian, or fresh cyclamen.

Inhale the fresh, biting scent of crushed rue leaves to clear your head in love matters of all sorts, especially to kill off any regret or hurt you may feel afterward.

Other herbs often carried to forget a lover are purslane, chicory, and honeysuckle.

Then, when the hurt has faded, make up a new love sachet and carry it with you, keeping in mind that old occult proverb that the death of love or any kind of death signals not the end, but merely the beginning of something even greater.

9

Herbs of the Elements and Magical Fluid Condensers

Witches believe that the elements are the building blocks of the universe. Everything that exists is made up of one or more of the four elements of air, fire, water, and earth. Even though this is understood today in the symbolic rather than literal sense, the system works and many Witches and magicians tap these powers to aid them in their magic.

One of the easiest ways to do this is through the use of fluid condensers. The fluid condenser is a magically charged infusion. It is one of the most effective methods of capturing, concentrating, and storing the innate powers of herbs.

Some magical herbalists in fact, use fluid condensers in nearly all of their magic, finding them the most effective of their magical tools. Others bolster their magic with fluid condensers but do not rely on them exclusively.

There are three basic types of fluid condensers: the *liquid* fluid condensers, the *solid* fluid condensers, and the *aeriform* fluid condensers. Of these, there are two methods of making them, the *simple* (one-substance) and the *compound* (two or more).

A word should be said about the *fluids* these condensers are named for. The universal forces are divided up by Witches even further than the elements into two poles: the electric and the magnetic. The electric is hot, fiery, active, masculine, and pursuing. The magnetic is cool, watery, passive, feminine, and attracting. This system is akin to that of the eastern yin/yang, the concept of total polarity.

Those materials that have been found to accumulate and retain these fluids are known as fluid condensers, since they *condense* and concentrate the forces.

Metals, oils, resins, tinctures, extracts, blood, and so on are all fluid condensers. The liquid fluid condensers are those in a liquid form, and these are the ones herbalists most often use in their work.

The well-stocked magical pantry includes four fluid condensers, one for each of the four elements, as well as a compound mixture for high-power rituals.

Following is a list of the various types of rituals and spells and their elemental rulers. For example, if you wished to use a fluid condenser to banish an illness, the fire fluid condenser would be the correct choice.

Types of Rituals and their Elemental Rulers

Earth: Fertility, jobs, promotions, money, business, investments, material objects, agriculture, health foods, ecology, conservation, stock market, antiques, old age, museums, buildings, construction, progress.

Air: Schooling, memory, intellectualism, teaching, tests, divination, communications, travel, writing, organizing and organizations, groups of all kinds, theorizing, drug addiction.

Fire: Success, sex, banishing illnesses, the military, conflicts, protection, courts, law, police and sheriff's agencies, contests, competitions, private detectives, dowsing, treasure hunting, gambling, athletics, strength, good health, war, terrorism.

Water: Love, friendships, partnerships, unions of every kind, affection, contract negotiations, beauty, rest, recuperation, meditation, spirituality, healing wounds, restoring cell growth, childbirth and children, the home, receptivity, family, swimming and scuba diving, fishing, ancestors, medicine, hospitals, compassion, doctor and nursing professions, clairvoyance.

Appropriate herbs and plants to be used for each type of condenser:

EARTH

Balm of Gilead

Bistort

Cedar

Cinquefoil

Cypress

Fern

High John the
    Conqueror

Honeysuckle

Horehound

Jasmine

Mandrake

Patchouli

Pine

Sage

Slippery elm

Air

Acacia

Anise

Benzoin

Broom

Comfrey

Elder

Eucalyptus

Eyebright

Hazel

Lavender

Lemon verbena

Marjoram

Mastic

Mistletoe

Mugwort

Nutmeg

Peppermint

Pimpernel

Sandalwood

Spearmint

Thyme

Wormwood

Fire

Alder

Angelica

Basil

Bay laurel

Betony

Carnation

Celandine

Cinnamon

Clove

Coriander

Garlic

Heliotrope

Holly

Hyssop

Juniper

Marigold

Mullein

Nettle

Oak

Pennyroyal

Peony

Pepper

Primrose

Rosemary

Rowan

Rue

Saffron

St. John's wort

Thistle

Tobacco

Vanilla

Vervain

Water

Apple

Ash

Burdock

Camomile

Camphor

Catnip

Cucumber

Cyclamen

Elecampane

Gardenia

Geranium

Hawthorn

Heather

Henbane

Hops

Hyacinth

Ivy

Lettuce

Lovage

Meadowsweet

Myrrh

Myrtle

Sweet orange

Orris

Pansy

Periwinkle

Poppy

Rose

Star anise

Violet

Willow

Yarrow

Basic Fluid Condenser Process

Follow this procedure to make any of the elemental fluid condensers.

Take two handfuls of the fresh or dried herb (use only one herb, or a combination) and put it into your pot. Pour pure, cold water over it so that the herb is covered. Cover the pot and boil the herb over flame for about twenty minutes (it is okay to check a clock). Cool, without removing the lid, for thirteen minutes. Strain the liquid, then return it to the pot and boil until it is halved in quantity. Leave the lid on during the processes, but check it every few minutes to see how it is progressing.

Let cool, covered, and then add the same amount of spirits (gin or vodka work well) or fuel alcohol. Now, shake the condenser vigorously, then strain again through four layers of fine linen into a small dark-glassed bottle and cork it. Store in a cool, dark place until needed.

To add extra potency, some magicians add a little of their own blood to the mixture, just after adding the spirits. Or, some add a small piece of gold, which is then filtered out and retrieved. These substances add extra potency to the fluid condensers, though they are certainly not necessary. Store the liquid fluid condenser where the Sun's rays will not reach them, in a dark-glassed bottle that is tightly corked.

Remember, make the condenser with the proper herbs of the element, and be sure when making compound condensers that an odd number of plants are used. Label the bottle carefully so that there will be no question later as to whether it is an air or fire condenser.

Using the earth condenser: Take a quantity of the earth fluid condenser, a few teaspoons will do, and pour it into a glazed earthenware bowl. Load this with your desire, then throw it onto the earth, preferably outside of the city. Roadsides and pathways are to be avoided at all costs.

As the earth soaks up the condenser, call out your desire, and visualize your wish. Only when the liquid has been completely absorbed is the spell finished.

If you live in the city and cannot find an appropriate place to do this, it is permissable to use a flower pot.

Naturally there are many other ways of using this condenser: anoint the wallet or money to attract prosperity, wear when asking for a promotion or raise, etc.

Using the air condenser: Get a small, metal bowl or saucer. Pour some spring water into it, then add three drops of the air fluid condenser. Now, holding the bowl in both hands, close your eyes and concentrate, very hard, upon your desire. See your intent as if it has already been made manifest. Load the fluid condenser with your desire.

Concentrate on the object while holding it in your hands—*feeling* that you are infusing it with your desire, visualizing magnetic force from your body entering into and charging the object with power until it seems as if it can hold no more.

Place the bowl or saucer onto a flame, gas, or spirit, or hang over a fire and let the liquid evaporate. As it rises into the air, wave your magic knife or wand through the steam, calling upon the powers of that element to help you in making your intent a reality. When the liquid is completely evaporated, the spell is finished.

Naturally, there are many other ways to use this condenser. Students may wish to anoint the forehead with the air fluid condenser to aid in their studies. If a person has come to you for help in overcoming drug addiction (or any other kind of bad habit) use the condenser to anoint the person, or give him a small vial of the liquid and give him instructions to anoint the soles of his or her feet, hands, back of the neck, and forehead.

The list of appropriate rituals to be performed with the air fluid condenser should give ample ideas.

Using the fire condenser: Cut a piece of white, clean paper, four inches square, with your magic knife. Write upon it your intent in red ink (the red ink corresponds to the fire element). Moisten the paper with a few drops of the fire fluid condenser and allow this to dry.

When it is dry, load the paper with your intent, then burn the paper. The best results will be obtained if the paper can be instantly and completely consumed in the heat of a large fire or furnace. If not, however, the flame of a candle will do. During the combustion, concentrate upon your intent. When the paper is totally consumed the forces will be set in motion.

This condenser must never be allowed to touch the skin. If you are using it to heal illnesses, anoint healing sachets or banishing candles, but never the patient's bare skin. This is an excellent aid for all types of banishing rituals (spirits, garden and house pests, sicknesses, unhealthy or harmful habits, etc.).

Using the water condenser: Take a new glass jar and go to a place that has running water, such as a river, stream, or spring. It is best if the river flows from east to west. Without being watched, fill the container with water and then take it to a secluded area nearby, where you will not be seen. For even more effective results, use water that has been gathered from three different sources.

Pour a few drops of the water fluid condenser into the water and let it mix well together. Next, perform the intent-infusing, loading with your desire.

When this is done, throw the water (but not the jar) into the river and call upon the forces of waters of the earth to aid you in the spell, visualizing the thing desired as having happened.

The water condenser is marvellous for anointing love sachets, marriage charms, and for adding to beauty and love baths.

The compound fluid condenser: Sometimes known as the *universal fluid condenser,* this mixture is highly appropriate for all types of spells and is used to give an added boost of power. It is an excellent general anointing liquid for charms and amulets, magical tools, and sachets, and is used, too, in purificatory baths and washes. Candles, magical images, jewelry, and precious stones all are aided and powered by the regular application of this liquid. Use your imagination in finding new uses. It is made as follows:

Angelica leaves

Sage leaves

Cucumber skin

Camomile flowers

Oak leaves or bark

Violet flowers or leaves

Peppermint leaves

Tobacco leaves

Melon seeds

Take equal parts of each of these, about two handfuls, and put into your pot. Cover them with spring water and boil slowly for half an hour. Cool, strain, and boil until the mixture becomes thick. Now, as with the elemental condensers, add the same amount of spirits. Add a few drops of blood, or a piece of gold if you wish to. Shake the mixture well, strain again (if you have added the gold and blood), then pour into a dark-glass bottle. Store in a cool, dry place, and be sure the label contains all important data, including the date of composition.

Needless to say, all work in the manufacture of condensers is best performed while the Moon is waxing. The day and planetary hour are not important, as these are general-use tools.

Condensers can be powerful aids to tapping the powers of the elements, if they are made with care and used with a good deal of faith and imagination.

10

Scented Oils
and Perfumes

The use of scented oils and perfumes is inextricably
bound up with Witchcraft, magic, and occultism.
Magical oils are used to concentrate the powers of an
herb, flower, tree, or root much the same way as fluid
condensers.

But the greatest value of oils is that they retain the
full scent of the plant. And scents have powerful reactions upon the human intellect and emotions, even the
body itself.

In Witchcraft, oil is a symbol of the element of fire,
much as incense symbolizes air, and salt the earth. The oils
capture, draw out, and store the essential nature of herbs
and flowers, the basic energies that the old Witches called
the *fiery being.*

Their magic works through vibrations and scent. The vibratory rate of an herb, oil, or incense determines whether
it is beneficial or destructive, and the degree thereof.

These vibrations are then broken down into subcategories. Those that are *loving* herbs and *prosperity* herbs, and so on.

All herbal magic works through vibrations. The magic of oils, however, also uses the olfactory sense in manifesting change. Scents trigger various centers in the brain and bring them into dominance. Thus, lilac oil stimulates the *psychic* center and helps develop clair-voyant powers. Other centers include the *intellectual, spiritual, passionate,* and so on.

Oil and perfume magic is a science that takes years to fully master. Anyone, however, can use oils in their magic following simple instructions.

The oils described in this chapter are to be used with caution and a sense of fair play. Wearing a seductive scent or a heady cologne is fine, but purposely trying to seduce someone through a fragrance is bordering on manipulation. Use your good sense of judgment when using these oils.

Some of these oils can be prepared at home for a fraction of what they cost in the stores. Naturally, the homemade ones are not of the same high quality, but the genuine, natural essential oils of some herbs and flowers are costly; many currently sell on the market for well over one thousand dollars an ounce.

Reliable mail-order companies selling essential oils are noted in appendix 3.

Making the Oils

The simplest method is known as *enfleurage.* Fill a small jar with the leaves and petals of the herb(s) you wish to make an oil from. (Dried herbs will do if the fresh are not available.) Next, pour olive oil over them to cover. Tightly cork or cap the jar and keep in a warm place (out of sunlight) for three days. Shake the bottle each day to thoroughly wet the leaves.

On the third day strain the oil, fill the jar with fresh leaves or flowers, and pour the same oil back into the jar. Repeat several times until the oil is heavily saturated with the fragrance.

Finally, strain the oil through filter paper or a piece of fine muslin and store in a tightly stoppered bottle, opaque being the best.

Some herbalists add a few drops benzoin tincture to the oils as a preservative. To make benzoin tincture, soak one tablespoon powdered benzoin in one-fourth cup good-quality vodka or apple cider vinegar for three weeks. Strain and keep tightly corked in a dark bottle.

The most propitious day upon which to make oils depends upon the type of oil but, since several days usually elapse during the manufacture of an oil, it is best to make the oil when the herbs and flowers are available, and if you wish, later dedicate it on the day and in the hour of the planet involved.

Oil Blessing

Dip the blade of your knife into the oil, then raise it to the sky and say:

In the name of the Moon,
of the stars, and of the Sun,
I bless this oil.

This blessing may be used with any of the oils listed in this chapter.

For making blends of oils, get some good, glass jars in which to blend the oils. Have your eyedropper ready to add the oils a drop or two at a time. In fact, if you have several droppers available, use all of them, one for each scent that you are blending. Keep a jar of alcohol nearby to clean the droppers.

Fragrance blending is an acquired art, and takes a keen sense of smell and vibrational content. With practice it comes easier.

Following are recipes for oil blends often used in magic.

Anointing Oil

These are all-purpose anointing oils, often worn during spell-casting and other magic pastimes. Their ancestors are the infamous *flying ointments* of the Persecution times (for more on these flying ointments, see appendix 2).

Literally dozens of variations exist. Sometimes vervain oil is used alone, but usually in combination with other herbs. Here are a few examples (feel free to experiment):

All-Purpose Anointing Oils

Vervain	Frankincense
Cinquefoll	Myrrh
Parsley	Benzoin

Carnation	Ambergris
Frankincense	Civet
Sandalwood	Musk

Patchouli

Ambergris

Musk

Frankincense

As always, the artificial ambergris, civet, and musk scents may be used, as the natural are quite expensive and usually unavailable. Besides, they are taken from animals. Remember, *harm none!*

These are very powerful and worth the time and trouble it takes to make them. The first recipe can be made by the enfleurage method, the rest are best made by blending the already made (or store bought) oils.

There are thirteen traditional anointing points upon the body, and these are used when a very heavy aura of protection and psychic energy is desired around the body.

The anointing must be done nude, usually directly after the ritual purification bath. Dab a bit of the oil on the soles of the feet, the bend of the knees, the genitals, the base of the spine, the wrists, over the heart, the breasts, under the chin, and on the forehead.

Such an extensive anointing procedure should be undergone only when performing a full-fledged magical ritual, and even then it is not entirely necessary. If you wish, just dab a little on the wrists and forehead.

Love Oil

On a Friday evening when the Moon is waxing, gather a little ground orris root, an earthen bowl, and a quantity of pure olive oil. If you are a woman also have a vial of jasmine oil; patchouli will do for men.

Lay a pink cloth on the altar. Light pink candles. Pour the orris root into the earthen bowl, then add about half a cup of olive oil. Stir with the forefinger of your strong hand seven times clockwise. Now add the essential oil, no less than three drops, no more than seven.

Place the bowl on the altar. Gaze into it, infusing the oil with your desire for love. Enchant it by saying:

Love, love, love, love, love, love, love.

Simple and to the point, right? You might want to substitute a favorite love poem or sonnet.

Pour the oil into a jar and cork it tightly. Leave in a dark space, surrounded by the pink altar cloth, for seven days. Upon the next Friday night, uncork the bottle, strain, and then store in the same bottle until needed. Love oil should only be worn by its creator.

Protection Oil

To make a personal protection oil, blend together the oils of rosemary, rose geranium, and cypress. This oil is also used to anoint candles and is added to protective cleansing baths.

Handfasting Oil

A handfasting is a Witch's wedding ceremony. This oil, however, can be used by any couple regardless of their marital status. It is one of the few magical oils that contains a dried herb mixed in with the essences.

This is often given to Witch couples on the evening of their handfasting. The formula:

Gardenia, for peace and harmony

Musk, for passion and courage

Jasmine, for continuing love

Rose geranium, for protection against adversity

Blend together (using the eyedropper, a drop at a time) until the scent seems perfect. Make up two ounces or so. Then add one pinch dried yarrow. Yarrow is used in love and marriage spells since it has the power to keep a couple together for seven years. Seven is the number of Venus, the planet of love.

When finished, pour into twin crystal jars. One of these is given to the woman; the other to the man. For seven nights, the couple should anoint one another, using their own jars. Then the oils should be blended together, poured into one of the jars, and the other jar should be hidden in some secret place.

Satyr Oil

A famous controversial oil, there are several variations in the recipe, but all are very earthy and passionate fragrances. The man who wears this should be prepared for anything!

Start with a base of musk and patchouli. Add cinnamon, carnation, and vanilla oils. Blend and add until the scent seems right to you. Blend on Tuesday.

This oil should only be worn by men. It does not always smell great, but it works as an aphrodisiac and the results can be quite amazing!

Fragrance of Venus Oil

For women who wish to become more attractive (absolutely magnetic) to men, wear this oil.

On a Friday night blend together jasmine, red rose, a drop of lavender (no more!), a bit of musk, and ylang-ylang oils.

This oil should only be worn by women who are wishing to attract men.

Four Winds Oils

East Wind, the wind of intelligence: lavender

South Wind, the wind of passion and change musk

West Wind, the wind of love and the emotions: rose

North Wind, the wind of riches: honeysuckle

Wear the appropriate oil when desiring a change in that area of your life. Also, wear to boost spells you may be working.

South Wind is the catch-all; if your wish does not fall into any of the other categories, use South Wind.

Following is a guide to the most-used magical oils. This does not include the so-called *brand name* magical oils, nor the *voodoo* blends sometimes sold in occult shops. These are the raw ingredients, from which many oils can be made. Feel free to blend and mix your own private oils.

Scented Oils and their Magical Powers

Acacia: Possessing high spiritual vibrations, this oil is worn to aid meditation and to develop psychic powers. Some also use it to anoint their altars, censers, and candles.

All-spice: Very vitalizing. Gives added determination and energy, excellent for convalescents. Anoint daily.

Almond: Almond oil, the symbol of wakefulness to the ancient Egyptians. Is used in prosperity rituals (anointing candles, money, etc.), and also added to money incenses.

Anise: A boon to clairvoyance, it is often added to a ritual bath preceeding any attempt at divination. It is also worn during divinatory rituals.

Apple blossom: Wear to promote happiness and success. Anoint candles during love rituals. Add to bath to aid relaxation.

Basil: The scent of basil causes sympathy between two people so wear to avoid major clashes. It creates harmony of all kinds. Prostitutes used to wear it in Spain to attract business. The home. Brings luck to your home and gold to your pocket. A magnetic oil to be worn by men.

Benzoin: This oil brings peace of mind. It is used in purification ceremonies. A drop or two smouldering on a charcoal block will effectively clear the area with billowing clouds of smoke.

Bergamot: Used in protective rituals and also in drawing prosperity. Wear on the palm of each hand.

Camphor: Wear to strengthen psychic powers. Also anoint yourself when you have decided to break off with a lover, or when they have done so with you and you find it hard to let go.

Carnation: This is an oil of power. It is used as an energy restorer after exertion, as an aid to healing, and in consecration ceremonies. Should be worn when extra energy for a ritual is desired.

Cinnamon: A high-vibration oil, used for personal protection. It is also a sexual stimulant in the female. Added to any incense, it increases its powers. Mixed with powdered sandalwood, it makes an incense suitable for all religious or spiritual magic. Good for meditation, illumination, and so on.

Cinquefoil: Protective, strengthens the five senses. Also *five lucks*—love, money, health, power, and wisdom— so is often used to anoint amulet and charm bags.

Clove: An aphrodisiac, worn to attract lovers. Inhaled, the oil helps the memory and eyesight.

Coriander: A love oil used to anoint candles.

Cumin seed: Brings peace and harmony to the home. Anoint all doorways once a week just before sunrise when the household is asleep and all is quiet.

Cyclamen: Worn to ease childbirth by the expectant mother. Also used in love and marriage spells.

Cypress: An oil of blessing, consecration, and protecttion. It is a symbol of the earth element, as well as of death. When attending a funeral of a friend or loved one, wear this oil so that you will be uplifted by the meaning of death as the doorway to but another life. It also effectively screens out the negative vibrations of the mourners. Wear on Samhain to become aware and remember those who have passed on.

Eucalyptus: A healing oil, very useful in recuperation after long illnesses. Cures colds with daily application to the throat, forehead, and wrists, and by adding it to healing baths. Also used for purifications.

Frankincense: One of the most sacred of all oils, used to anoint magical tools, the altar, etc. A strong purifier used in exorcisms, purification rituals, and blessings.

Gardenia: Wear to attract love. A powerful feminine magnetic oil. Protective.

Ginger: A tropical aphrodisiac. Induces passion.

Heliotrope: High spiritual vibrations, drenched with the energies of the Sun. Aids in clairvoyance.

Honeysuckle: An oil of the mind, it promotes quick thinking and is often used as a memory aid by dabbing on the temples. Also used in prosperity rituals.

Hyacinth: Brings peace of mind to the mentally disturbed. A very relaxing oil.

Hyssop: Increases finances, and is added to the bath to create a purifying atmosphere. An excellent oil to wear during all types of magical rituals.

Jasmine: Symbol of the Moon, and of the mysteries of the night. Jasmine oil is used to attract love. The scent helps one to relax and sleep. It also facilitates child-birth. It is sometimes used for meditation and general anointing purposes. This is a purely spiritual oil.

Lavender: Used in healing and purifying rituals, and also to arouse sexual desire in men. Prostitutes wore it extensively to advertise their trade and to attract customers.

Lemon grass: An aid to the psychic powers. Wear on the forehead. Spiritualists and mediums use it, for it helps make contact with spirits.

Lilac: Induces far memory, the act of recalling past lives. It is also useful in inducing clairvoyant powers in general. Brings peace and harmony.

Lotus: The sacred oil of the ancient Egyptians. Lotus oil has a high spiritual vibration and is suitable for blesssing, anointing, meditation, and as a dedicatory oil to your god(s). It is also used in healing rituals. One who wears lotus oil is sure of good fortune and much happiness.

Magnolia: An excellent oil for meditation and psychic development. It also brings peace and harmony.

Melilot: Fights depression, or what the old Witches used to call *melancholy.*

Mimosa: Used in healing rituals, and also in producing prophetic dreams. Anoint the forehead before retiring.

Mint: Used in prosperity spells, and to increase one's business. Anoint wallets, etc.

Musk: The universally accepted *sex scent*. It is also worn to purify and to gain courage. It is a magnetic oil. Worn with equal success by both sexes. *Note:* The musk oil sold through most reputable dealers is a blend of other oils and not of true musk. The authentic musk is prohibitively expensive, as it is obtained only from the musk deer. Some musk oils are synthetic, but, again, it is not always the substances which produce the scent that matter, but the scent itself.

Myrrh: A purification, protection, and hex-breaking oil. Possesses a high vibratory rate, making it excellent for the more religious rituals of magic. Anoint the house every morning and evening as a part of any protection ritual.

Narcissus: *Stupifyer.* This oil brings peace and harmony. Soothes the nerves and relaxes the conscious mind. A narcotic-type oil.

Neroli: Magnetic women's oil. Rubbed between the breasts to attract men, or onto the temples to give peace.

New-mown hay: This scent is available from Aphrodisia in New York. It is an excellent oil to wear when making a great transformation in your life. Turning over a new leaf, starting a new project.

Nutmeg: This oil is rubbed onto the temples and the third eye to help in meditation and to induce sleep. It is protective as well.

Orange blossom: To make a person in the mood for marriage, wear this oil. Many women add it to their daily baths to build up their attractiveness. Sometimes known as *mantrap*. Enough said!

Orris root: Attracts the opposite sex. Douse your clothes with the oil.

Patchouli: A very powerful occult oil; one of the magnetic oils to be worn by men. It attracts women. Also wards off negativity and evil, gives peace of mind, and is very sensual.

Peony: A lucky scent for all who need customers, success in business, or good fortune.

Peppermint: Used to create changes within one's life. Also used to relax and allow one to "unwind."

Rose: The love oil. Used in all love operations, added to baths, and to induce peace and harmony. Take a handful of rose buds, place them in a silver goblet. Pour one dram rose oil over them. Let soak for a week. After this, on a Friday night. Burn them over the charcoal to infuse your house with loving vibrations. This is an excellent *peace* incense, and can be done regularly to ensure domestic tranquility.

Rose geranium: Oil of protection. Anoint window sills, doors of house. Wear on self. Also imparts courage to the wearer. An excellent oil to use to bless a new home or apartment. A few drops on a charcoal block will release its powerful vibrations throughout the entire house. Also used to anoint censers.

Rosemary: A very vitalizing oil, rosemary is used in healing rituals and also to promote prudence, common sense, and self-assurance. It aids mental powers when rubbed onto the temples. It is also protective and is used much like rose geranium. Rub onto the temples to ease pain of headache and in all healing rituals.

Rue: To break up negativity and curses, anoint a sprig of dried rue with this oil. Tie up in a red bag and carry for protection. Add nine drops of the oil to the bath every night for nine nights in succession during the Waning Moon to break a spell that has been cast against you. Salt may be added to the bath as well.

If a magical image has been found, a poppet, or fith-fath, this is what you must do: do not touch it, or allow others to touch it. Get a bottle of rue oil (keep some handy for this purpose) and drench the doll with the oil, making sure that the whole image is covered with the oil. Then light the whole thing on fire (even clay dolls, the clothes, or just the oil itself should light) saying a banishing rune such as the following (insert your own deities, names):

Thy power spent, thy form in flames,
Be banished by the great god's names!

If this is impossible to do where the doll is lying, because of danger of the fire spreading, nosy neighbors, or whatever, move the doll without touching it, using a wooden stick, to a safe place, outdoors, then douse and burn. The oil breaks the spell and the burning of the doll symbolizes the spell going to ashes. While the doll is burning you must visualize the spell's defeat, using, say, a huge wall made up of great stone blocks. See the wall begin to topple and crash to the earth by the force of your counterspell. Firmly visualize this as the doll burns.

The one in whose name the doll was made is in no danger if this procedure is followed, nor is the sender of the spell. Never pick up or touch any strange image, charm bag, amulet, or even coin left near your home where it might have been purposely laid for you to find it. Such things are often loaded with negativity that is released when you touch it.

Rue is an excellent personal protection oil, but sometimes sets up violent allergic reactions in people. If you are sensitive to strong oils, do not wear this scent.

Saffron: Wear to aid in the development of clairvoyant powers.

Sandalwood: Protective, very healing, this oil is used to anoint. It also aids one in seeing past incarnations. Try anointing the forehead to promote *the second sight.*

Sesame: Gives hope to one who is sick, discouraged, or lonely.

Sweet pea: One of the most beautiful of all scents, sweet pea oil is worn to attract strangers of all kinds, some of whom may become lovers or friends. Wear as a personal oil.

Spikenard: Wear during rituals to the ancient deities of Egypt, also to anoint sacred objects, such as altars, tools, etc.

Tuberose: Mistress of the night, as it is also known, is an excellent aphrodisiac. Promotes peace and also aids in psychic powers. Men wear it to attract women. Very much a physical oil.

Vanilla: A vitalizing oil, said to be sexually arousing in women. Use as an energy restorer. Sometimes used to gain extra power during magical ceremonies.

Vervain: Assists in obtaining material objects. It also stimulates creativity. Aids those who desire success in the performing and creative arts.

Violet: The oil is used in love operations and is sometimes sexually exciting. However, many people can't stand the fragrance of the violet, for some curious reason. Once thought to be sacred to the fairy queen (i.e., the goddess of the Witches). Very healing, added to baths.

Wisteria: The door between the world of humans and the realms of the gods, the passport to higher consciousness. Wisteria is used to contact other planes of consciousness and existence, and to bring illumination. Wear only when in complete serenity.

Ylang-ylang: Makes its wearer irresistible to the opposite sex. Also soothes the problems of married life. Can help in finding a job. If worn to interviews you will be much calmer and more impressive to the interviewer. Sometimes called *flower of flowers*.

11

Incenses

S weetly scented smoke, spiraling upward to the stars, Sun, and Moon, is an almost universal feature of magical altars. It is linked with magic and religion as far back as can be traced. The earliest Witches and magicians threw fragrant herbs and woods onto fires or glowing embers to release their scents. In later times, cauldrons and censers contained these charcoal blocks, and the ritualistic burning of incense became an established part of magical and religious practice.

The power of incense lies in its vibrations and scent. Be warned, however, that many herbs smell vastly different when they are being burned or fumed than in their natural states. In most mixtures, it is not the scent that is important but the vibrational rate it emits while being smoldered on the charcoal in the censer.

Incense is used today to cleanse and purify magical tools and working areas, to raise vibrational rates and summon energies, to banish and exorcise evil entities and influences, to concentrate and contain power, and to build up an atmosphere attuned to the type of ritual to be performed.

Incense is available commercially from many herb stores, religious supply outlets, and occult shops. The most powerful and effective incense, however, is that which you concoct yourself. Store-bought incense works, of course, but not as well as homemade.

The basic form of the incense used in magic is the granulated, or raw form. This is also the most complicated to work with. Cone, stick, or block incense is complete in and of itself, but the granulated or powdered form must be smoldered on glowing charcoal blocks within a censer or some other device capable of holding red-hot coals.

This can be a very showy part of a ritual, with the use of censers, clouds of scented smoke, and a good deal of symbolic carrying or swinging of the censer.

As an aid to magic, incense ought to be prepared with care and serious intent, observing proper days and phases of the Moon for best results. The ingredients are easily purchased from the usual sources, either in your town or by mail.

Your mortar and pestle will come in handy in their manufacture, for many gums and woods have to be ground to a fine powder, and the final blend will need to be mixed together.

Though many of the herbs are available in preground form, it is best to grind them yourself, if you have the time. The repetitive action of the pestle moving within the mortar, and the time involved in silently (or invokingly) mixing up these age-old incenses increases their power. Use your own judgment when purchasing ingredients whether to buy preground or not.

When actually mixing up the incense, enchant it by saying a little rune stating the ultimate use of the scent. For instance, for an incense of purification, say something like, "Purify, purify, evil thou shalt deny," or simply state, over and over again, the basic use of the incense.

Following are a few recipes themselves. These, together with the others described elsewhere throughout this book, should give you a good idea of the methods of creating blends and also their basic uses.

Before using any incense, perform an exorcism over it. Set it on the altar between two burning white candles, either still in the mortar, or in a bowl. Touch the center of the incense with the tip of your magic knife and, summoning all your willpower and energy, say in a forceful voice:

I conjure thee, by this sign,
to drive out all that is impure and unclean,
so that thou mayest receive
strength, virtue, and power.
May this incense be a boon and
an aid in the magical art,
and serve me well.

As usual, you may add any names of gods or goddesses you hold sacred, such as Diana, Tara, Jesus, etc.

Now the incense is ready for use in your magical art. It is best to perform this exorcism on the Full Moon or a few days afterward.

When finished, store the incense in a dark-glassed or ceramic jar with a tight stopper. Keep from light and, if it is not completely used up within a year, lay in a fresh batch.

Incenses of Purification and Exorcism

These incenses dramatically raise the vibratory rate of a room or building so that negativity and evil is driven out. Such incenses are often praised for their *cleansing* and *clearing* powers.

Perhaps the most powerful of all purificatory incenses is frankincense, a gum from a tree that grows in eastern countries and has been used in religious rituals for centuries.

This is practically an all-purpose incense, used for purification, exorcism, and all manner of banishing rituals. It is the basic ingredient in many incenses.

In purifying a large area, frankincense is sometimes set fuming on several censers placed in different areas of the house or building, though one is generally enough. Objects that are to be purified (old jewelry, coins, amulets, etc.) are held in the smoke for several seconds.

Used alone it is quite powerful, and there is no need to add any other herbs.

Protection Incenses

At times, an additional magical protection may be desired, especially when performing very heavy magical operations or when there is a serious disturbance in your neighborhood, such as a rash of burglaries or violence.

These incenses set up an impenetrable barrier surrounding you and your space, effectively turning away harmful energies, thoughts, and physical threats. (Although you should have the locks checked and take all the normal precautions as well. Magic works with you, and not for you; always back it up with physical actions that will help bring about your intent.)

A good protection incense can be compounded of frankincense, sandalwood, and rosemary. Alternately, any of the herbs listed in chapter 5 can be burned, singly or in combination.

Here is a selection of incenses with varied uses. If you wish to alter a formula, do so as long as the change is made with wisdom and thought.

Moon Magic

Mix together equal parts of these herbs: Add one-quarter part orris root. Anoint with a few drops of lotus oil. Burn during the Full Moon to receive its blessings and during all lunar rituals.

Success Incense

Equal parts of:

Cinnamon

Benzoin

Mix, grind together, and burn when you desire success in the business world.

Yule

Burn during all winter rites, and also to purify the home from November 1 to March 21:

> Pine
>
> Juniper
>
> Cedar

Offertory

Often burned as a *sacrifice* or as a general working blend. Use when no other incense seems to be right for the ritual.

Equal parts:

> Rose petals
>
> Vervain
>
> Cinnamon
>
> Myrrh
>
> Frankincense

Meditation Incense

A good blend:

> Bay leaves
>
> Sandalwood
>
> Damiana

Burn a little at a time; do not set too much smouldering on the coals directly before going into meditation.

Kyphi

An ancient Egyptian blend often used in general magical working, and especially burned at night. Plutarch
said, "Its aromatic substances lull to sleep, allay anxi-
eties, and brighten the dreams. It is made of things that
delight most in the night and exhibits its virtues by
night." It is also a useful banishing incense.

On the night of the New Moon, get about half a
handful raisins and put them into an earthenware bowl.
Cover with white wine and let steep, loosely covered in
a place where they can remain undisturbed for five days.

Three nights after setting the raisins to steep, take
equal parts of the following herbs:

> Juniper
>
> Sweet sedge root
>
> Acacia
>
> Henna

Macerate in white wine and steep all that night and
the next day, until night falls again. On this night, just
as the Sun sets, if possible, gather together these dried
herbs:

> Calamus
>
> Gum mastic
>
> Cinnamon

Peppermint

Galangal

Bay laurel

Orris

Take equal parts of each and grind well until it is the consistency of a powder. Mix well and set aside.

Now mix together one tablespoon each powdered myrrh and honey. Add to this the drained raisins, and drained herbs, and finally work in the powdered herbs. If the texture is too dry to mix completely, add a little of the used white wine.

Spread out on a wooden board and let dry, uncovered for some time. Then pack into jars. This is a wonderful scent, useful in all magical operations.

Study Incense

Burn, while studying, to increase mental powers and concentration efforts, and also to improve the memory.

Equal parts:

Cinnamon

Rosemary

Mace

Burn only a small amount at a time.

Circle Incense

For general magical work, this formula is well suited and very helpful in raising power:

Frankincense, two parts

Myrrh, one part

Benzoin, one part

Cinnamon, one part

Rose petals, two parts

Vervain, one part

Rosemary, two parts

Sandalwood, one part

Bay laurel, one part

All herbs should be finely powdered and mixed until completely blended. (*Note:* It is nearly impossible to powder bay leaves completely. Even in the modern grinders and electric processors they just do not reduce to a powder. So, add the bay leaves and do not worry about the lumps that will remain when you've finished powdering the rest. Rose petals are sometimes a problem, too, as is frankincense—the latter sticking to the pestle. Remember, though, the energy you exert in the composition of the incenses is directed into them, and thusly, they will be of greater power.)

Planetary Incense

This incense is aptly named, for it contains ingredients sacred to each of the planets. Burn for extra power during rituals.

Frankincense, Sun

Orris root, Moon

Lavender, Mercury

Rose petals, Venus

Dragon's blood, Mars

Cinquefoil, Jupiter

Solomon's seal, Saturn

Mix up, with fairly equal parts. (There are many varieties of dragon's blood. Be sure to research all of them. Some are harmful and can cause pregnant women to abort.)

Prosperity Incense

Equal parts:

Cloves

Nutmeg

Lemon balm

Poppy seed

Cedar

Moisten with a few drops each of:

Honeysuckle oil

Almond oil

Make on a Thursday during the Waxing Moon.

Love Incense

Mix on a Friday during the Waxing Moon:

Rose petals

Patchouli

Cinnamon

Red sandalwood

Burn during rituals designed to draw love to you.

© Robin Wood 1986

12

Amulets

Herbs are often worn or carried in order to tap their specific powers. Following are several traditional herbal amulets, some of which are questionable, some fanciful, but all fascinating and potentially useful.

To see ghosts: Carry lavender and inhale its scent.

To allay fear: Carry a mixture of nettle and yarrow.

To detect witches: Carry a sachet of rue, maiden-hair, agrimony, broom-straw, and ground ivy.

To be courageous: Wear a fresh borage flower, or carry mullein.

To avoid military service: Wear the four-leaved clover if you wish to avoid duty.

To ensure safety and protection on a journey: Comfrey worn or carried will safeguard you.

To prevent storms and wreckage while at sea: Put a garlic clove in your purse or in your pocket. In the South Pacific or in Hawaii wear a garland of *ti* leaves.

To guard against rape: Wear the heather to avoid all acts of passion.

To keep one from dreaming: Hang a sprig of lemon verbena around the neck.

To conceive: Wear the mistletoe, the cyclamen, or the bistort.

To prevent weariness while walking: Put mugwort in the shoe.

To keep venemous beasts and wild animals afar: Wear avens or mullein.

To keep others from deceiving you: Wear the pimpernel or snapdragon.

To keep disease afar: Wear a sprig of rue around the neck. (Rue can cause dermatitis.)

To enable a soldier to escape his or her enemies: Wear the vervain and you shall accomplish this.

To avoid being sent to the gallows: Wear or carry a carnation.

To ensure victory: Wear woodruff to win.

To ensure that friendly words are spoken to you: Wear the heliotrope.

To enter the underworld: Carry an apple, or the branch of an apple tree that bears buds, flowers, and fully ripened fruit.

To regain lost manhood: Carry an acorn or mandrake root.

To remain youthful: Carry an acorn.

To prevent drunkeness: Wear a chaplet of saffron, crocus, parsley, or rue to prolong your enjoyment. (Rue can cause dermatitis.)

To see faeries: Gather wild thyme and carry it with you, or put it on the eyelids (with your eyes closed) and sleep on a faerie hill.

To be a successful fisherman: Carry a bit of the hawthorn.

To see a unicorn: As this beast usually lives among ash trees, carry a bit of the wood or leaves and you may see one. Or lie down among ashes and place one of its leaves on your chest and wait for one to make itself known.

13

Witch's Herbal

This section is an alphabetical listing of the herbs commonly used in magic. It is by no means complete, in the number of herbs included or in the uses thereof, but it should serve as a reference guide when devising your own spells and rituals.

For this reason, all extraneous wording and information has been omitted. The format provides clear and easy access to the common name, Latin name, folk and magical names, gender, ruling planet, ruling element, parts used, basic powers, and specific uses of a wide variety of herbs. Also included are deities associated with the herbs.

Some of this information may take a bit of explanation. The *gender* of an herb, for instance, refers to the type of energy the plant emits. If a plant's influence is stimulating, aggressive, electric, and/or positive, it is *hot*. Plants that are relaxing, passive, magnetic, and/or negative are *cold*.

Herbs are also sometimes classified as being *masculine* or *feminine,* but I prefer the hot-cold method as it does not bring up the question of sexism.

The Latin and folk names are given to help in distinguishing one herb from another, as many have similar names but quite different properties.

Most of the rest of the information is self-explanatory. Keep in mind, though, that this list could be expanded a hundred-fold and still not begin to record all the magical powers of herbs. It should be used as a guide on the path of magical herbalism. When there is a question of when to use one herb over another, use your intuition.

You will note the absence of medicinal or medical information. I have purposely left this out, as there are a number of reliable guides in this area.

Acacia *(Acacia senegal)*

Folk names: Cape gum, gum arabic tree, Egyptian thorn

Gender: Hot

Planet: Sun

Element: Air

Associated deities: Osiris, Astarte, Ishtar, Diana

Parts used: Twigs, wood

Basic powers: Protection, clairvoyance

Specific uses: Burn with sandalwood during meditation, to seek illumination, and to develop the psychic powers. Carry the wood as a protective amulet.

Anemone *(Anemone pulsalilla)*

Folk names: Wind flower, pasque flower

Gender: Hot

Planet: Mars

Element: Fire

Associated deities: Adonis, Venus

Part used: Flowers

Basic powers: Healing

Specific uses: Healing charms, amulets. Gather a perfect bloom when the first are seen in spring, tie up in a red cloth, and carry as a guard against disease.

Angelica *(Angelica archangelica* or *A. officinalis)*

Folk names: Masterwort, archangel, garden angelica

Gender: Hot

Planet: Sun

Element: Fire

Associated deity: Venus

Parts used: Leaves, root

Basic powers: Protection, exorcism

Specific uses: Grow in garden as a protection. Carry the root with you as an amulet. Burn the dried leaves in exorcism rituals.

Anise *(Pimpinella anisum)*

Folk names: Anneys, aniseed

Gender: Hot

Planet: Jupiter

Element: Air

Part used: Seeds

Basic powers: Protection, purification

Specific uses: A good, general cleansing bath is made with a handful of anise seeds and a few bay leaves. This is especially effective if you have (accidentally or intentionally) killed something. A pillow of anise keeps away all nightmares.

Apple *(Pyrus malus)*

Folk names: Fruit of the underworld, silver bough, tree of love, silver branch

Gender: Cold

Planet: Venus

Element: Water

Associated deities: Venus, Hercules, Diana, King Arthur, Dionysius, Olwen, Apollo, Hera, Athena

Parts used: Fruit, cider, blossoms

Basic powers: Love, healing

Speciflc uses: Add apple blossoms to love and healing incenses. Cut an apple in three pieces, rub each on a sick person's body, and then bury them. The decaying apple will cure the illness. The same ritual is done with warts. Pour cider to give life to a newly dug field. Give an apple to a lover as a present, cut it in half, and eat one half while your lover eats his or hers. Use apple cider in place of blood or wine, if they are called for in old magical spells and rites. Eat apples on Samhain. Apples are sometimes also used in place of the poppet.

Asafoetida *(Ferula foetida)*

Gender: Hot

Planet: Saturn

Element: Fire

Part used: The herb

Basic powers: Exorcism, purification

Specific uses: This acrid herb is burned or carried to drive away evil and disease. Destroys manifestations. Keeps fever and colds away if worn.

Ash *(Fraxinus excelsior* or *F. americana)*

Folk name: Nion

Gender: Hot

Planet: Sun

Element: Water

Associated deities: Poseidon, Woden, Thor, Mars, Gwidion, Neptune

Parts used: Leaves, branches

Basic powers: Protection

Specific uses: Carve some of the wood into an equal-armed cross as a protection against drowning. The Witch's broom is made from an ash staff, together with birch twigs and a willow binding. Magic healing wands are often made from ash branches. If mandrake is not available, poppets are carved of ash roots to be used in healing and other rituals. Place ash leaves beneath the pillow to induce prophetic dreaming. Use in sea rituals of all kinds.

Avens *(Geum urbanum)*

Folk names: Herb bennet, star of the earth, yellow avens, bennet, blessed herb, golden star

Gender: Hot

Planet: Jupiter

Element: Fire

Part used: The herb

Basic powers: Protection

Specific uses: Carry as an amulet to guard against wild animals. Burn during exorcism and cleansing rituals. Add to protective sachets, amulets, and incenses.

Balm of Gilead *(Populus candicans)*

Folk name: Mecca balsam

Gender: Cold

Planet: Saturn

Part used: Buds

Basic powers: Protection, intellectual, manifestations

Specific uses: Carry the buds to mend a broken heart. Burn to set up a material basis in which spirits may manifest during ceremonies of this kind. Add to love and protection sachets.

Basil *(Ocimum basilicum)*

Folk names: American dittany, alabahaca, St. Joseph's wort, sweet basil, Witches' herb, our herb

Gender: Hot

Planet: Mars

Element: Fire

Associated deities: Krishna, Vishnu

Part used: The herb

Basic powers: Purification, protection, exorcism, love

Specific uses: Add to exorcism and protection incenses. It is an ingredient of the purification bath sachet. Often used in wealth and prosperity rituals. Add to love sachets and incenses.

Bay Laurel *(Laurus nobilis)*

Folk names: Bay, bay tree, Greecian laurel, Indian bay, Roman laurel, sweet bay, baie

Gender: Hot

Planet: Sun

Element: Fire

Associated deities: Aesculapius, Apollo, Ceres, Cerridwen

Part used: Leaves

Basic powers: Protection, clairvoyance, exorcism, purification, healing

Specific uses: Burn the leaves to induce visions. Wear as an amulet to ward off negativity and evil. Burn and scatter on the floor in exorcism and purification rituals. Put leaves under the pillow to induce inspiration and prophetic dreams. Add to purification incenses and baths. Use in healing incenses and sachets. Pick while facing east, just at sunrise. Protection against lightning.

Benzoin *(Styrax benzoin)*

Folk names: Benjamen, gum benzoin, Siam benzoin

Gender: Hot

Planet: Sun

Element: Air

Part used: Gum

Basic powers: Intellectual, purification

Specific uses: Burn with cinnamon for business success. Use in purification incenses to clear the surrounding area. A tincture of benzoin is used to preserve magical oils.

Betony *(Stachys officinalis)*

Folk names: Bishopwort, lousewort, wood betony, purple betony

Gender: Hot

Planet: Jupiter

Element: Fire

Part used: The herb

Basic powers: Protection, purification

Specific uses: Add to all incenses of purification and protection. Burn in outdoor fires and jump through the cleansing smoke, especially at Midsummer. Stuff a pillow with the herb and sleep on it to prevent nightmares. Carry to protect against intoxication.

Bistort *(Polygonum bistorta)*

Folk names: Patience dock, snakeweed, dragonwort, sweet dock, osterick, passions, English serpentary, red legs, Easter giant

Gender: Cold

Planet: Saturn

Element: Earth

Part used: The herb

Basic powers: Clairvoyance, fertility

Specific uses: Carry it if you wish to conceive. Add to divinatory incenses, especially with frankincense.

Broom *(Cytisus scoparius)*

Folk names: Link, genista, banal, scotch broom, Irish broom

Gender: Hot

Planet: Mars

Element: Air

Part used: The herb

Basic powers: Purification, protection, wind spells

Specific uses: Use the plant to sweep the surrounding area when working magic outside. Use in purification incenses and hang a little of the herb in your magic room as a protection. Use to raise and calm winds. Raise them by throwing the herb into the air, preferably off a mountain top, and calm them by burning the herb.

Bryony *(Bryonia alba)*

Folk names: Wood vine, briony, tetterberry, white bryony, tamus, ladies' seal, wild hops, wild vine

Gender: Hot

Planet: Mars

Element: Earth

Part used: Roots

Basic powers: Prosperity, protection

Specific uses: Bryony roots are often used in place of the rather rare mandrake root. A bryony root is set on a piece of money to cause one's riches to grow.

Burdock *(Arctium lappa)*

Synonyms: Beggar's buttons, clotburr, bardana, happy major, hardock, burrseed, personata, great burdock, hurrburr, cocklebur

Gender: Cold

Planet: Venus

Element: Water

Part used: The herb

Basic powers: Purification, protection

Specific uses: Cast in house or magic room to ward off negativity. Add to protection sachets of all kinds. Wear a necklace of dried, carved burdock roots as protection against magic.

Cactus (all species)

Gender: Hot

Planet: Mars

Element: Fire

Parts used: Whole, living plant, spines

Basic powers: Protection

Specific uses: Grow in the garden and inside the house as a safeguard against burglary and un-wanted intrusions. Grow in the bedroom to guard your chastity. The spines are used in image magic, to mark or write symbols on images of wax or roots.

Such uses are usually restricted to the more negative aspects of image magic, however. Fill a jar with cactus spines, rusty nails and old tacks, pins and needles. Add rue and rosemary leaves to fill the jar, seal tightly, and then bury under your doorstep as a powerful protective device.

Camomile *(Anthemis nobilis)*

Folk names: Maythen, manzanilla, chamaimelon, camamyle, ground apple, whig plant, Roman camomile

Gender: Hot

Planet: Sun

Element: Water

Part used: Flowers

Basic powers: Prosperity, meditation

Specific uses: Use in prosperity charms to draw money. Add to incenses intended to bring on restful states for meditation. Induces sleep if burned.

Camphor *(Cinnamomum camphora)*

Gender: Cold

Planet: Moon

Element: Water

Part used: Gum

Basic power: Anaphrodisiac

Specific uses: Endeavor a would-be lover to smell camphor if he or she is forcing their attentions on you and you are not interested. It will instantly turn him or her off. Used also in incenses to produce sleep. Worn in a small pouch around the neck, it wards off colds.

Caraway *(Carum carvi)*

Folk names: Careum carvi

Gender: Hot

Planet: Mercury

Element: Air

Part used: Seeds

Basic powers: Protection, passion

Specific uses: Carry and use in sachet bags for protection. Add to love sachets and charms to attract a lover in the more physical aspect of that word. Carry the seeds to strengthen the memory. Once used to cure fickleness in lovers.

Carnation *(Dianthus caryophyllus)*

Folk names: Nelka, gilliflower, Jove's flower

Gender: Hot

Planet: Sun

Element: Fire

Part used: Flowers

Basic powers: Protection, energy

Specific uses: Once worn by Witches to prevent untimely death on the scaffold, it is used in power incenses and placed on the altar to produce added energy. Dry nine red carnations in the Sun, crumble them, and separate from the stems. Pour one dram carnation oil over them, mix well, and smolder on charcoal for a tremendously powerful incense. Produces tons of energy!

Catnip *(Nepeta cataria)*

Folk names: Field balm, catmint, catnep, cat's wort, nip, catrup

Gender: Cold

Planet: Venus

Element: Water

Associated deity: Bast

Part used: The herb

Basic powers: Love, animal contacts

Specific uses: Dry large leaves to use as bookmarks in magical books. Give to your cat to sniff and play with and to create a psychic bond between you and your cat. Use in love sachets and incenses, especially with rose petals.

Celandine *(Chelidonium majus)*

Folk names: Tetterwort, garden celandine, greater celandine, chelidonium, devil's milk, swallow herb, swallowwort, celydoyne

Gender: Hot

Planet: Sun

Element: Fire

Part used: The herb

Basic powers: Protection, escape

Specific uses: Aids in escaping unwarranted imprisonment and entrapments of every kind. Wear next to skin and replace every three days. Imparts joy and good spirits if worn and it cures depression.

Cinnamon *(Cinnamonum zeylanicum* or *C. lauraceae)*

Folk names: Sweet wood, cassia

Gender: Hot

Planet: Sun

Element: Fire

Part used: Bark

Basic powers: Protection, healing, passion

Specific uses: Burn to raise very high spiritual vibrations. Use in healing incenses and burn to stimulate clairvoyance. One of the herbs used to stimulate and excite the passions of the male. Add to prosperity mixtures. Mix with myrrh for a good incense for general working.

Cinquefoil *(Potentilla canadensis)*

Folk names: Five-finger grass, five-finger blossom, sunfield, synkefoyle, five fingers

Gender: Hot

Planet: Jupiter

Element: Earth

Part used: The herb

Basic powers: Protection, love, prosperity, healing

Specific uses: Hang at door as a protecton. Use in all spells of prosperity, purification, and protection. Cinquefoil represents love, money, health, power, and wisdom, and so is an all-purpose magical herb. To make a good prosperity sachet, mix together equal parts of cinquefoil, cinnamon, cloves, lemon balm, and add a whole vanilla or tonka bean. Do this on a Thursday after sunset during

the Waxing Moon. Sew up into a rich purple
cloth bag and carry to increase riches.

Clove *(Caryophyllus aromaticus* or *Syzygium aromaticum)*

Gender: Hot

Planet: Sun

Element: Fire

Part used: Flower buds

Basic powers: Worn to drive away hostile and negative forces, and to stop gossip.

Specific uses: Carry to strengthen the memory and
add to sachets designed to attract the opposite
sex. A necklace of cloves (string them on a red
thread, using a needle) is often given to babies as
a protective device. Hang where they will not be
able to touch it.

Clover *(Trifolium* spp.)

Folk names: Trefoil, honeystalks, three-leaved grass

Gender: Hot

Planet: Mercury

Element: All four elements

Part used: The herb

Basic powers: Protection

Specific uses: The three-leaved clover is often used in rituals designed to protect or to keep one looking youthful and fair. As a protection, carry one on your person. To keep looking young, gather dew on May Day morning, just before the Sun rises. Put into this water three clover stalks. Let these steep all day out of the Sun's rays. The next morning, again before the Sun rises, rub a little of the water on your face. Do this every morning until the water is used up. Cover the bowl with a cloth to keep the water clean and store in a place where it will remain untouched until the following morning.

Four-leaved clovers are carried to prevent madness. It is also a popular amulet to avoid military service. Gather the four-leaved clovers in the morning, then walk to the nearest hill. As the Sun rises, throw one clover to the north, and one to each of the other directions, calling upon the powers of the elements to protect you, to keep you from getting drafted, or whatever your wish is. Then, after finishing the ritual, pluck one more four-leaved clover (remember, leave something in payment to the earth for the plant taken) and keep it as a magical link with the elements. Snakes will not venture where clover grows.

Comfrey *(Symphytum officinale)*

Folk names: Yalluc, slippery root, boneset, assear, consolida, healing herb, guni plant, consound, bruise wort, knitbone wallwort, black wort, healing blade, salsify

Gender: Cold

Planet: Saturn

Element: Air

Part used: The herb

Basic powers: Protection

Specific uses: To ensure your safety while traveling, carry some comfrey. Put some in your luggage to ensure *its* safety!

Coriander *(Coriandrum sativum)*

Folk names: Cilentro, cilantro, culantro, Chinese parsley

Gender: Hot

Planet: Mars

Element: Fire

Part used: Seeds

Basic power: Love

Specific use: Long used in love sachets and charms.

Cucumber *(Cucumis sativus)*

Gender: Cold

Planet: Moon

Element: Water

Part used: Fruit

Basic powers: Healing, fertility

Specific uses: Bind peel around head to cure headache. Add seeds to lunar incenses. The cucumber aids fertility if kept in the bedroom. Replace every seven days.

Cyclamen *(Cyclamen europaeum)*

Folk names: Sow bread, groundbread, swinebread

Gender: Cold

Planet: Venus

Element: Water

Associated deities: Hecate, Venus

Part used: The herb

Basic powers: Love, fertility, protection

Specific uses: Grow in the bedroom as protection while sleeping. Carry the blossoms to remove the grief of an ended love affair. Grow outside to protect the garden and the house. Carry the flower to aid in fertility matters.

Cypress *(Cupressus* spp.)

Folk name: Tree of death

Gender: Cold

Planet: Saturn

Element: Earth

Associated deities: Mithras, Aphrodite, Ashtoreth, Pluto, Persephone, Hercules, Saturn

Parts used: Branches, wood

Basic powers: Protection, consecration

Specific uses: Make a fire of cypress and consecrate ritual objects in its smoke. Hang up for protection. Add to incenses used during the Waning Moon, or during the magical season of winter. Carry with you to become illuminated concerning death in all its aspects.

Dill *(Anethum graveolens)*

Folk names: Dill weed, aneton, dilly, garden dill

Gender: Hot

Planet: Mercury

Element: Fire

Part used: The herb

Basic powers: Protection, love

Specific uses: Use in love sachets. Tie up dried seed heads as protection. Hang in cradle to protect children. Also use in protection sachets and incenses. Add a half-handful of dill seeds to your bath water to attract women to you.

Dragon's Blood *(Daemonorops draco* or *Dracaena draco)*

Gender: Hot

Planet: Mars

Element: Fire

Part used: Gum

Basic powers: Energy, purification, protection

Specific uses: Add a pinch of the ground herb in incenses to increase their potency and effectiveness. Add to love incenses and sachets. Put a piece of dragon's blood under the mattress to cure impotency.

Elder *(Sambucus canadensis)*

Folk names: Yakori bengestro, devil's eye, lady elder, frau holle, rob elder, hollunder, ellhorn, pipe tree, boure tree, bour tree, sweet elder, tree of doom, old lady, battree, old gal

Gender: Cold

Planet: Venus

Element: Air

Associated deities: Holda, Venus

Parts used: Leaves, berries, flowers

Basic powers: Purification, love

Specific uses: Scatter berries and leaves to the four winds to protect. The branches are often used for fashioning magic wands. Stand beneath the elder and you will never be struck by lightning. (It is not advisable to stand beneath any tree during a lightning storm.)

Elecmapane *(Inula helenium)*

Folk names: Scabwort, nurse-heal, elfwort, aly-compaine, elfdock, horse-heal

Gender: Hot

Planet: Mercury

Element: Water

Parts used: Root, leaves

Basic power: Love

Specific uses: Add to love charms of all kinds, especially in conjunction with mistletoe and vervain.

Eucalyptus *(Eucalyptus globulus)*

Folk name: Blue gum

Gender: Cold

Planet: Moon

Element: Air

Part used: Leaves, pods

Basic powers: Healing

Specific uses: Stuff healing poppets and pillows with the leaves. Ring blue candles with eucalyptus leaves and burn for healing vibrations. Hang a branch of eucalyptus leaves over the sickbed or in the sickroom, or add a few leaves to flowers sent to the afflicted. String immature (green) pods and hang around the neck to cure colds and sore throats.

Eyebright *(Euphrasia officinalis)*

Folk names: Euphrosyne, red eyebright

Gender: Hot

Planet: Sun

Element: Air

Part used: The herb

Basic power: Clairvoyance

Specific uses: Brew a simple and anoint the eyelid daily to induce clairvoyant visions. Use in making magic condensers for general magic work. (Caution: can cause dim vision.)

Fern (All spp.)

Gender: Hot and cold, depending

Planet: Saturn

Element: Earth

Part used: The herb

Basic powers: Protection, love

Specific uses: All ferns give extremely powerful protection. Grow in shady areas of the garden and in the house. Always include in vases of flowers. Throw fern on hot coals to send up an aura of protection. Also burn out-of-doors to bring rain. The unexpanded fronds of the male fern are dried over a Midsummer fire and kept for protection. These *lucky hands* are rare nowadays.

Frankincense *(Boswellia carterii)*

Folk names: Olibanum, olibans, incense

Gender: Hot

Planet: Sun

Element: Fire

Associated deities: Ra, Baal

Part used: Gum

Basic powers: Protection, purification, consecration, exorcism

Specific uses: Burn to raise vibrations, purify, consecrate, protect, and exorcise. Often used in charm bags and sachets. Induces visions and aids meditation. Burn during sunrise rituals of all kinds. Mix with cumin and burn as a powerful protective incense useful for general working.

Gardenia *(Gardenia* spp.)

Gender: Cold

Planet: Moon

Element: Water

Part used: Flower

Basic powers: Love passion

Specific uses: Wear the flower to attract love and new friends. Also wear the fresh flower to attract lovers. Dry and crush its petals. Mix with ground orris root and lightly dust the body to attract the opposite sex. Use as a link with the Moon.

Garlic *(Allium Sativum)*

Folk Name: Poor man's treacle, garleac, garlicke, clove garlic

Gender: Hot

Planet: Mars

Element: Fire

Associated deity: Hecate

Part used: Bulb, flower

Basic powers: Protection, exorcism

Specific uses: Take garlic with you on trips over water to prevent drowning. Sailors carry it with them on board to prevent wreckage of the ship. Peel cloves of the fresh bulb, and place one in each room when disease threatens. Italians once bit the herb when evil spirits surrounded them, or when they feel fearful. Hang up in newly built homes. The flowers are often used to decorate protective altars. Add to all protective sachets, hang up a rope of garlic in the kitchen. Also, use in exorcisms. Mountain climbers carry to keep fair weather on their expeditions.

Geranium *(Geranium* spp. and *Pelargonium* spp.)

Gender: Cold

Planet: Mars

Element: Water

Part used: Flowers

Basic powers: Love, healing, protection

Specific uses: Wear the flowers or add them to love sachets. The white variety is worn to promote fertility, while the red are a good protection and aid healing. Plant the flowers in the garden (especially the pink and red) to protect the house and to keep snakes away from your property.

Hawthorn *(Crataegus oxyacantha)*

Folk names: Huath, May bush, tree of chastity, thorn, white thorn, May

Gender: Hot

Planet: Mars

Element: Fire

Associated Deity: Cardea

Parts used: Leaves, wood

Basic power: Protection

Specific uses: Make an anti-lightning charm of the wood. Tie up leaves in protection sachets. Carry to ensure good fishing. Witches often danced beneath hawthorns in England, and they still do.

Hazel *(Corylus* spp.)

Folk name: Coll

Gender: Hot

Planet: Sun

Element: Air

Associated deities: Mercury, Thor, Artemis, Diana

Parts used: Nuts, wood

Basic powers: Fertility, protection, mental powers

Specific uses: Hazel wood makes good all-purpose wands. The forked branches are used in divining hidden objects, especially those buried in the earth. String hazel nuts and hang up in the house for luck. Present brides with a bag of the nuts to ensure luck and fertility, or carry one to make yourself fertile. The wood serves as an anti-lightning charm. The nuts are eaten to gain wisdom. Tie two hazel twigs together with red or gold thread to form a solar cross for a good-luck charm. Gather at night on Samhain. Draw a circle around yourself on the ground with a hazel twig if outside and in need of magical protection.

Heather *(Calluna vulgaris)*

Folk names: Common heather, ling, Scottish heather

Gender: Cold

Planet: Venus

Element: Water

Associated deity: Isis

Part used: The herb

Basic powers: Protection, rain-making

Specific uses: Carry as a guard against rape. Burn with fern to attract rain.

Heliotrope *(Hellotropium europaeum* or *H. aborescens)*

Folk names: Turnsole, cherry pie

Gender: Hot

Planet: Sun

Element: Fire

Associated deity: Apollo

Parts used: Flowers, leaves

Basic powers: Clairvoyance, exorcism

Specific uses: Put under the pillow to induce prophetic dreams, especially to discover the thief when you have been robbed. Also used in exorcism, incenses, and healing sachets.

Henbane *(Hyoscyamus niger)*

Folk names: Hog's bean, devil's eye, henbells, Jupiter's bean, poison tobacco

Gender: Cold

Planet: Saturn

Element: Water

Part used: Leaves

Basic power: Love

Specific uses: Gathered by a naked man, standing on one foot, alone, in the morning, it will help him gain the love of a woman, for it makes its bearer pleasant and *delectable*. Sometimes thrown into water to make rain. Do not eat!

High John the Conqueror *(Impomoea purga)*

Folk name: Jalap

Gender: Cold

Planet: Saturn

Element: Earth

Part used: Root

Basic power: Prosperity

Specific uses: Anoint the root with mint oil and tie up in a green or purple bag to attract needed money. Also, add the root to candle-anointing oils.

Holly *(Ilex aquifolium* or *I. opaca)*

Folk name: Tinne

Gender: Hot

Planet: Mars

Element: Fire

Part used: The herb

Basic power: Protection

Specific uses: Tie up as an anti-lightning charm. Heightens masculinity if one carries a sachet filled with the leaves and berries. Holly planted outside around the house is a good protection. An attractive protective plant to be used in decorations at Yuletide.

Honeysuckle *(Lonicera caprifolium)*

Folk name: Woodbine

Gender: Hot

Planet: Jupiter

Element: Earth

Part used: Flowers

Basic powers: Prosperity, clairvoyance

Specific uses: Ring green candles with the flowers to attract money. Add to all prosperity sachets. Lightly crush the fresh flowers and rub on the forehead to heighten clairvoyance powers.

Hops *(Humulus lupulus)*

Folk name: Beer flower

Gender: Hot

Planet: Mars

Element: Water

Part used: Fruit

Basic power: Healing

Specific uses: Healing incenses and sachets. A pillow stuffed with the dried herb helps bring on sleep.

Horehound *(Marrubium vulgare)*

Folk names: Eye of the star, white horehound, hoarhound, maruil, soldier's tea, seed of Horus, bull's blood, marrubium, haran haran, llwyd y cwn

Gender: Hot

Planet: Mercury

Element: Earth

Associated deity: Horus

Part used: The herb

Specific uses: Protective sachets, incenses.

Hyacinth *(Hyacinthus orientalis)*

Gender: Cold

Planet: Venus

Element: Water

Part used: Flowers

Basic powers: Love, protection

Specific uses: Sachets to ease childbirth, protection, and a guard against nightmares. Sniff the fresh flower to relieve grief.

Hyssop *(Hyssopus officinalis)*

Folk names: Ysopo, isopo

Gender: Hot

Planet: Jupiter

Element: Fire

Part used: The herb

Basic powers: Purification, protection

Specific uses: Add to purification bath sachets of all types, protection sachets, and incenses.

Ivy *(Hedera* spp.)

Folk name: Gort

Gender: Cold

Planet: Saturn

Element: Water

Associated deities: Bacchus, Osiris, Dionysus, Cerridwen

Part used: The herb

Basic power: Protection

Specific uses: A guardian when growing on the walls of a house or other building. Ivy is magically married to holly, and the two are often given to newlyweds. Used in primitive orgiastic rites of Bacchus and Dionysius.

Jasmine *(Jasminum officinale* or *J. odoratissimum)*

Folk names: Moonlight on the grove, jessamin

Gender: Cold

Planet: Jupiter

Element: Earth

Part used: Flowers

Basic powers: Love, prosperity

Specific uses: The flowers are used in love sachets and in prosperity rituals of all kinds. Jasmine attracts spiritual love.

Juniper *(Juniperus communis)*

Gender: Hot

Planet: Sun

Element: Fire

Basic powers: Protection, love

Specific uses: A sprig of juniper will protect the wearer from accidents. One of the earliest incenses used by Witches was made from a combination of the leaves and the dried, crushed berries. String the matured berries for an attractive charm, designed to attract lovers. Sometimes used in anti-theft sachets, as it guards against thieves. Grow juniper at your doorstep for protection.

Lavender *(Lavendula officinale* or *L. vera)*

Folk names: Spike, elf leaf

Gender: Hot

Planet: Mercury

Element: Air

Part used: Flowers

Basic powers: Love, protection, purification

Specific uses: An ingredient in the purification bath sachet, lavender is also used in purification incenses. It is thrown onto the Midsummer fires by Witches as a sacrifice to the ancient gods. Lavender is a frequent addition to healing sachets, especially bath mixtures, and is added to incenses to cause sleep. At one time lavender was carried with rosemary to preserve chastity. Conversely, it is widely used to attract men for sexual affairs. Carry the herb to see ghosts.

Lemon Verbena *(Lippia citriodora)*

Folk names: Yerba louisa, cedron

Gender: Cold

Planet: Venus

Element: Air

Part used: The herb

Basic powers: Protection, love

Specific uses: Wear to make oneself attractive to the opposite sex. A strengthening herb often added to charms to add extra power. Hang a sprig around your neck to stop you from dreaming.

Lettuce *(Lactuca sativa)*

Folk names: Sleep wort, garden lettuce

Gender: Cold

Planet: Moon

Element: Water

Part used: The herb

Basic powers: Rest, anaphrodisiac

Specific uses: Rub the juice of the herb onto the fore-head to induce sleep and relaxation. Protective if grown in the garden. If you are consumed with lust, eat the leaves to cool down if you wish to.

Lovage *(Levisticum officinale)*

Folk names: Love root, lavose, sea parsley, Italian parsley, loving herbs, love parsley, lubestico, levisticum, Chinese lovage

Gender: Hot

Planet: Sun

Element: Water

Part used: Root

Basic powers: Love, purification

Specific uses: Add the root to baths to become psy-chically cleansed. Also add to the bath with seven rose buds to make you more attractive to the opposite sex. Carry as a love attractor.

Mandrake, European *(Mandragor officinarum)*

Folk names: Brain thief, mandragor, alraun, gallows, mannikin, wild lemon, racoon berry, herb of Circe, baaras, womandrake

Gender: Hot

Planet: Mercury

Element: Earth

Associated deities: Hecate, Hathor

Part used: Root

Basic powers: Protection, fertility

Specific uses: Place in the home as a powerful protective charm. Women carry the root to help them conceive. The root is used in image magic, but as the true mandrake is exceedingly rare the roots of the bryony or ash are good substitutes. In America, the May apple *(Podo phyllum peltatum)* is considered a fair replacement for the mandrake, and is often called *American mandrake.* Small bits of the genuine root, which are occassionally available in herb stores, are added to sachets for protection. The root is carried by men who wish to cure their impotency. Both types of mandrake, when available whole, are placed on the altar and the hearth as protective devices.

Marigold *(Calendula officinalis)*

Folk names: Calendula, summer's bride, husband-man's dial, holigold, marybud, marygold, bride of the Sun, pot marigold, spousa solis, golds, gold

Gender: Hot

Planet: Sun

Element: Fire

Part used: Flowers

Basic powers: Love, clairvoyance

Specific uses: Place the flower beneath the head at night to induce clairvoyant dreams. A vase of these flowers in any room immediately brings a renewed surge of life to everyone in it. Sometimes added to love sachets. It should be gathered at noon.

Marjoram *(Origanum majorana)*

Folk names: Joy of the mountains, marjorlaine, wintersweet, sweet marjoram, knotted marjoram, majorane, pot marjoram, mountain mint

Gender: Hot

Planet: Mercury

Element: Air

Associated deities: Venus, Aphrodite

Part used: The herb

Basic powers: Protection, love

Specific uses: Add to all love charms. Place a bit of the herb in every room of the house for protection. This should be changed every month. Give to a grieving person to draw happiness into their life. Infuse marjoram, rosemary, and mint, and use this liquid to sprinkle protective vibrations around the house, and also to cleanse physical objects.

Mastic *(Pistachia lentiscus)*

Folk names: Masticke, gum mastic

Gender: Hot

Planet: Sun

Element: Air

Part used: Gum

Basic powers: Clairvoyance, manifestations

Specific uses: Add to incenses where a manifestation is desired. Burn also to gain *the sight.*

Meadowsweet *(Filipendula ulmaria)*

Folk names: Little queen, queen of the meadow, bridewort, gravel root, trumpet weed, lady of the meadow, steeplebush, bride of the meadow, meadsweet, dollor, meadowwort

Gender: Hot

Planet: Jupiter

Element: Water

Part used: The herb

Basic powers: Love

Specific uses: Arrange fresh meadowsweet on the altar when mixing up love charms and sachets. Also add to love and peace incenses and strew around the house. It possesses very gentle vibrations.

Mistletoe *(Viscum album)*

Folk names: Birdlime, donnerbesen, all heal, devil's fuge, thunderbesom, golden bough, European mistletoe

Gender: Hot

Planet: Sun

Element: Air

Part used: The herb

Basic powers: Protection, love

Specific uses: Pick on Midsummer's Eve, or when the Moon is six days old (i.e., six days after the New Moon). Wear as a protective amulet, or to help conceive. The wood is often carved into rings and other magical objects. A good anti-lightning charm. The herb hung anywhere is an excellent all-purpose protective device. Extinguishes fire. Wear as an amulet to preserve against wounds.

Mugwort *(Artemisia vulgaris)*

Folk names: Naughty man, old man, old uncle Harry, artemisia, artemis herb, Witch herb, muggons, sailor's tobacco, felon herb

Gender: Cold

Planet: Venus

Element: Air

Associated deities: Artemis, Diana

Part used: The herb

Basic powers: Protection, clairvoyance

Specific uses: Put into the shoe to prevent fatigue on long journeys. Carry to ward against wild beasts, poison, and stroke. Make a simple and drink it to induce clairvoyance. Rub the fresh young leaves on magic mirrors and crystal balls to strengthen their powers. Add to scrying, clairvoyance, and divination incenses. Pick before sunrise during the Waxing Moon, preferably from a plant that leans north. The plant's powers are strongest when picked on the Full Moon. (Mugwort can cause dermatitis.)

Mullein *(Verbascum thapsus)*

Folk names: Hag's tapers, torches, clot, feitwort, doffle, candlewick plant, Aaron's rod, Peter's staff, lady's foxglove, velvet plant, Jupiter's staff, shepherd's herb, old man's fennel, velvetback, flannel plant, hedge taper, blanket leaf, shepherd's club

Gender: Cold

Planet: Saturn

Element: Fire

Part used: The herb

Basic power: Protection

Specific uses: Carry to keep wild animals away from you while walking in the wilderness, camping, or backpacking. Wear to instill courage. Use as a substitute for candles (do not light them) when performing magic outside where no flames can be lit. The powdered leaves are known as *graveyard dust* and are acceptable to use when such is called for in old recipes.

Myrrh *(Commiphoria myrrha)*

Folk names: Karan, mirra balsom odendron, gum myrrh tree

Gender: Hot

Planet: Sun

Element: Water

Associated deities: Isis, Adonis, Ra, Marian

Part used: Resin

Basic powers: Protection, purification

Specific uses: Burn to purify and protect. The smoke is used to consecrate, purify, and bless objects such as rings, amulets, talismans, and ritual tools. The resin is burned during healing rituals and purifications. Often used in charm bags, especially with frankincenses. It is one of the standard magical herbs.

Myrtle *(Myrica cerifera or Myrtus communis)*

Folk names: Candleberry, waxberry, bayberry tree, wax myrtle

Gender: Cold

Planet: Venus

Element: Water

Associated deities: Artemis, Aphrodite, Hathor, Astarte, Ashtoreth, Venus, Marian

Part used: The herb

Basic powers: Love, fertility

Specific uses: This is one of the strictly love herbs. Wear a chaplet of fresh leaves while making love charms. Add to all love sachets. Myrtle wood is an excellent substance to make magic charms from. Carry the wood to preserve youthfulness.

Nettle *(Urtica dioica)*

Gender: Hot

Planet: Mars

Element: Fire

Part used: The herb

Basic powers: Protection, exorcism

Specific uses: Stuff a small cloth doll or poppet with nettles to remove a curse and send it back to the sender. Write on the doll the name of the sender (if you know it; if not, never mind) and then bury or burn it. Sprinkle the herb around the room to protect or to add to protection sachets. Burn during exorcism ceremonies.

Nutmeg *(Myristica fragrans)*

Gender: Hot

Planet: Jupiter

Element: Air

Part used: Seed

Basic power: Clairvoyance

Specific uses: Carry the nut to strengthen your own clairvoyant powers. Add sparingly to divinatory incenses. Carry to ward off rheumatism.

Nuts and Cones

Basic powers: Fertility, healing

Specific uses: All nuts are steeped in magic. While the acorn, hazel, and walnut are described in detail elsewhere in this chapter, a few general words on nuts and cones are appropriate.

Most nuts are used to increase fertility, to help conceive. While underpopulation is hardly a problem today, herbal magic is sometimes called upon to provide help where the medical profession can supply none.

Nuts have a wide variety of magical uses: buckeyes are carried to prevent rheumatism, almonds are eaten to prevent intoxication and to gain wisdom, and the brazil nut is carried to find love.

Cones of the evergreen trees are also useful in fertility magic. The hemlock cones are collected and dried in the autumn, then dipped in green wax, and strung into necklaces. The circular shape of the necklace itself is a fertility symbol. These necklaces are worn by women who wish to become pregnant. This ritual is performed in secret.

Oak *(Quercus alba)*

Gender: Hot

Planet: Sun

Element: Fire

Associated deities: Dagda, Dianus, Jupiter, Zeus, Thor, Hercules, Herne, Cerridwen, Cernunnos, Janus, Rhea, Cybele

Parts used: Leaves, wood, fruit (acorn)

Basic powers: Fertility, protection, longevity

Specific uses: The most sacred and royal of all the trees. Magical rites are often performed in groves of oaks, and the most powerful mistletoe grows on these trees. Burn oak leaves to purify the atmosphere. The wood makes excellent all-purpose wands. The acorn is a fertility nut of the highest powers, carried to help conceive and to promote sexual relations. It is also worn or carried to preserve youthfulness, and to ward off illnesses. Hung in windows, it protects the house.

Several hundred years ago, Witches wore necklaces of acorns to symbolize the fertile powers of nature. This was especially popular during the winter months, when such a reassurance was comforting among the deep snows. Men carry the acorn to increase their own sexual attractiveness and prowess, or to cure impotency. When you gather leaves, acorns, or branches, pour a libation of wine on the roots of the oak. Gather the acorns during the day, leaves and wood at night. Fell oaks only in the wane of the Moon.

Onion *(Allium cepa)*

Folk names: Yn-leac, oingnum, unyoun, onyoun

Gender: Hot

Planet: Mars

Element: Fire

Parts used: Bulb, flowers

Basic powers: Protection, purification, exorcism, healing

Specific uses: Place halved onions in rooms to absorb illnesses and diseases. Throw the onions away in the morning without touching them. Rub onion halves on afflicted parts of the body to remove the problem. Arrange the flowers in a vase for a protective, decorative bouquet. Rub the magic knife's blade with the onion to cleanse it. The onion is sacred to the Moon, and so is used in lunar rites. Often used in protective spells with garlic. Grow onions in the garden to protect it.

Orange, Sweet *(Citrus sinesis)*

Folk name: Love fruit

Gender: Hot

Planet: Sun

Element: Water

Parts used: Fruit, flowers

Basic power: Love

Specific uses: Add dried peel to love sachets and charm bags. The fruit, eaten, hinders lust. Add the fresh or dried blossoms to a bath to make one attractive. Orange juice is often drunk in libations during magical rituals in place of the more commonly used wine.

Orris *(Iris florentina* or *I. germanica)*

Folk names: Queen Elizabeth root, florentine iris

Gender: Cold

Planet: Venus

Element: Water

Part used: Root

Basic power: Love

Specific uses: Carry the root to find a loved one. Add powdered orris to love sachets and baths.

Add to lavender and rosebuds to make a sachet to lie among clothes, infusing them with the scent of love. Use in small quanties in love incenses to fumigate the house before dates.

Pansy *(Viola tricolor)*

Folk names: Garden violet, heart's ease, Johnny jumper, stepmother, love-in-idleness

Gender: Cold

Planet: Saturn

Element: Water

Part used: Flowers

Basic power: Love

Specific use: Carry to attract love.

Patchouli *(Pogostemon cablin* or *P. patchouli)*

Folk name: Pucha-pot

Gender: Hot

Planet: Sun

Element: Earth

Part used: The herb

Basic powers: Passion, love

Specific uses: Attracts women and men. Wear alone, or with other love herbs. Usually used in oil form. Also burned in clairvoyance and divination incenses.

Pennyroyal *(Mentha pulegium)*

Folk names: Squaw mint, run-by-the-ground, lurk-in-the-ditch, pudding grass, piliolerian, tick-weed, mosquito plant

Gender: Cold

Planet: Venus

Element: Earth

Part used: The herb

Basic powers: Protection, exorcism

Specific uses: Put in the shoe to prevent weariness. Add to summer incenses and to protection and exorcism blends.

Peony *(Paenoia officinalis)*

Gender: Hot

Planet: Sun

Element: Fire

Associated deities: Paeon, Apollo

Part used: The herb

Basic powers: Protection, exorcism

Specific uses: Dry the root, or several roots, and make into a necklace or bracelet. The roots may be carved into attractive shapes. This is very protective. Use the root in breaking any enchantment by hanging it around the neck of the ench-anted one. Burn the seeds during exorcism rituals. Hang up the root or burn it to stop storms.

Pepper *(Capsicum* spp.)

Gender: Hot

Planet: Mars

Element: Fire

Part used: Berries

Basic power: Protection

Specific uses: Use in charm bags and amulets for protection. Burn mixed with other herbs (such as rosemary, dill, etc.) to fumigate and exorcise a place. The smoke can sting the eyes, so light it and then vacate the premises. Carry the herb to protect the mind from envious thoughts.

Peppermint *(Mentha piperita)*

Folk names: Lammint, brandy mint

Gender: Cold

Planet: Venus

Element: Air

Part used: The herb

Basic powers: Healing, purification

Specific uses: Add to healing incenses and charms. Rub onto the patient, and, if possible, especially over the afflicted area. Also burn to cleanse the house in winter, and inhale the fragrance of the crushed leaves if you have trouble falling asleep.

Periwinkle *(Vinca major)*

Folk names: Devil's eye, joy on the ground, sorcerer's violet, great periwinkle

Gender: Cold

Planet: Venus

Element: Water

Part used: Flowers

Basic power: Protection

Specific uses: Hang up on the door to protect all within the building. Gazing upon it can help in restoring lost memory.

Pimpernel *(Pimpinella magna)*

Folk names: Greater pimpernell, pimpinella

Gender: Hot

Planet: Mercury

Element: Air

Part used: The herb

Basic power: Protection

Specific uses: Wear to keep people from deceiving you. Good to protect the home and to guard against illness. Rub your magic knife's blade with its juice.

Pine *(Pinus* spp.)

Gender: Hot

Planet: Mars

Element: Earth

Associated deities: Cybele, Venus, Attis, Pan, Dionysius

Parts used: Cone, nuts, needles

Basic powers: Fertility, purification

Specific uses: Burn the crushed and dried needles in the winter to purify the home. This is good when mixed with equal parts juniper and cedar. The cones are carried as fertility charms, and

the nuts eaten for this same reason. Pine branches are sometimes used to sweep the forest
floor before performing magic outside. Add the
crushed needles to the bath sachet for a good
winter magical cleansing bath. (Research your
pine varieties. White pine has no precautions.
Other varieties can cause dermatitis and/or
have oils that can be irritating when touched.)

Poppy *(Papaver* spp.)

Folk names: Head waak, blind buff

Gender: Cold

Planet: Moon

Element: Water

Associated deities: Hypnos, Somnos, Ceres

Parts used: Seeds, dried seed pods

Basic powers: Fertility, prosperity

Specific uses: Add the seeds to your food if you
   wish to become pregnant. Get a dried seed pod,
   cut a small hole in it to remove the seeds, and
   write a question on a small piece of yellow
   paper. Stuff the paper inside the pod and lay it
   beside your bed. Prophetic dreams may answer
   the question before morning. Carry the dried
   seed pod as a prosperity amulet, or use the
   seeds in prosperity amulets.

Primrose *(Primula vulgaris)*

Folk names: Butter rose, English cowslip, password

Gender: Cold

Planet: Venus

Element: Fire

Associated deity: Freya

Part used: Flower

Basic power: Protection

Specific uses: Plant in garden to protect, especially the blue and red primroses. Especially powerful planted in pots sitting on the front and back porches.

Rose *(Rosa* spp.)

Gender: Cold

Planet: Venus

Element: Water

Associated deities: Venus, Hulda, Demeter, Isis, Eros, Cupid, Adonis

Part used: Flowers

Basic powers: Love, fertility, clairvoyance

Specific uses: Wash your hands with rose water before mixing up love mixtures. (Rose water may be purchased commercially in gourmet food shops and herb stores.) Bear the buds if you would find a love. Drink of tisane of rose petals to produce clairvoyant dreams. Burn the petals in the bedroom prior to sleep and have a completely refreshing, wondrous night. The petals are often added to healing incenses and sachets. Scatter fresh rose petals in the bed chamber on your honeymoon. To really prove you love another, send him or her red roses, the flowers of love.

Rosemary *(Rosemarinus officinalis)*

Folk names: Dew of the sea, incensier, sea dew, rosmaris, rosmarine, rosemarie, guardrobe

Gender: Hot

Planet: Sun

Element: Fire

Part used: The herb

Basic powers: Purification, love, intellectual, protection

Specific uses: Add to all purification bath sachets, love incenses, exorcism mixtures, and protection incenses. Wear a chaplet of rosemary to aid the memory. Hung up it wards off thieves. It has connections with the sea and so is used in all sea rituals, as well as in sachets designed to

ensure a safe, easy passage on the water. A good
protective sachet for boat or ship passengers can
be made up of rosemary, garlic (to stop storms),
and mistletoe (to guard against lightning
storms). Make a simple of rosemary and use it
to cleanse the hands before working magic, if
you have no time for the regular ritual bath.
Drink rosemary tea just before a test or exam
to ensure that the mind is fully awake and
functioning. Include a sprig in protection sachets of all kinds. It is often used to form a
protection wreath. Burn rosemary and juniper
as a healing and recuperation incense.

Rowan *(Sorbus aucuparia)*

Folk names: Mountain ash, witchwood, quick-
bane, wild ash, witchen, witchbane, wicken
tree, wiky, wiggy, roynetree, whitty, wiggin ran
tree, roden-quicken-royan, sorb apple, roden-
quicken, delight of the eye

Gender: Hot

Planet: Sun

Element: Fire

Associated deity: Thor

Parts used: Wood, twigs

Basic powers: Protection, healing

Specific uses: Tie two twigs of rowan together with red thread for a good all-purpose charm. Use the rowan branches in divining water, as is often done with hazel wood. It is an excellent protection against lightning. It is sometimes used to make magic wands. Carry the wood with you as a good luck *god* (amulet). A necklace of the berries is very healing.

Rue *(Ruta graveolens)*

Folk names: Ruta, bashoush, German rue, garden rue, rewe, hreow, herbygrass, herb of grace, mother of the herbs

Gender: Hot

Planet: Sun

Element: Fire

Associated deities: Diana, Aradia

Part used: The herb

Basic powers: Protection, intellectual, exorcism, purification

Specific uses: A fresh sprig of rue dipped in spring water is an excellent sprinkler, perfect for consecrations, blessings, and healings. The herb was worn to guard against the plague, and is now added to health sachets and those designed to keep illness away. Smell the crushed, fresh herb to instantly clear the mind of envious thoughts, unrequited love, and egotism. The herb is used to still a painful love. Add to exorcism incenses and purification sachets. Used in spells of inertia, to get something moving.

Saffron *(Crocus sativus)*

Folk names: Autumn crocus, Spanish saffron

Gender: Hot

Planet: Sun

Element: Fire

Part used: Flowers

Basic powers: Purification, clairvoyance, healing

Specific uses: Make a tea and use to cleanse the hands before healing rituals. Burn the herb as a healing incense and add to healing mixtures. Drink the tea to induce clairvoyance. Sometimes used to raise the winds, by throwing it into the air from high places, or by burning it and watching the smoke rise into the air.

Sage *(Salvia officinalis)*

Gender: Hot

Planet: Jupiter

Element: Earth

Part used: The herb

Basic powers: Healing, prosperity

Specific uses: Add to healing and prosperity sachets, incenses, and amulets.

St. John's Wort *(Hypericum perforatum)*

Folk names: Herba jon, John's wort, fuga daemonum, goat weed, tipton weed, amber, klamath weed

Gender: Hot

Planet: Sun

Element: Fire

Part used: The herb

Basic powers: Protection, exorcism

Specific uses: Hang around the neck to ward off fevers. Burn to banish and exorcise spirits. Pass the herb through the smoke of the Midsummer Eve's fire and then hang up in the house as a protection. At one time this herb was held to the mouths of accused Witches to make them confess. Wear the herb to make you invincible in war and battles of all kinds. Bear St. John's wort to strengthen your own will.

Sandalwood *(Santalum album)*

Folk names: Santal, sandal, white saunders, yellow sandalwood

Gender: Cold

Planet: Moon

Element: Air

Part used: Wood

Basic powers: Protection, purification, healing

Specific uses: Add to healing incenses and burn as a good purifying agent in any room. Also used in making healing oils and incenses.

Slippery Elm *(Ulmas fulva)*

Folk names: Red elm, moose elm, Indian elm

Gender: Cold

Planet: Saturn

Element: Earth

Parts used: Leaves, bark

Basic power: Protection

Specific uses: Burn and use in charm bags to stop others from gossiping about you or your friends.

Snapdragon *(Antirrhinum majus)*

Gender: Cold

Planet: Venus

Element: Fire

Part used: Flowers

Basic power: Protection

Specific uses: If one is *spelled* or feels threatened outside, step on a snapdragon to avert the evil magic. Wear as a protective amulet, or put vases of snapdragons in the house if you feel the need. Carry with you to see through other people's deceit. Can also be used to counteract charms and spells laid by others by adding to incenses and oil mixtures.

Solomon's Seal *(Polygonatum multiflorum* or *P. odoratum)*

Folk names: Dropberry, sealwort, sealroot

Gender: Hot

Planet: Saturn

Element: Fire

Parts used: Leaves, roots

Basic powers: Purification protection

Specific uses: Add to incenses and sachets to protect. Scatter to the four winds. Add to incenses of exorcism or to cleansing mixtures.

Spearmint *(Menta spicata)*

Folk names: Garden mint, lamb mint, green spine, spire mint, our lady's mint, mackerel mint, brown mint

Gender: Cold

Planet: Venus

Element: Air

Part used: The herb

Basic powers: Healing love

Specific uses: Add to healing incenses and poppets. Especially for curing lung diseases. A good addition to love mixtures and sachets.

Star Anise *(Illicium verum* or *I. anisatum)*

Folk name: Chinese anise

Gender: Hot

Planet: Jupiter

Element: Water

Part used: Seed

Basic power: Clairvoyance

Specific uses: Burn the seeds as incense to bring
clairvoyance, or rise in making herbal pendulums. They are sometimes strung on a string
along with nutmegs, tonka beans, etc., to make a
magically charged (and very fragrant) necklace.

Sunflower *(Helianthus annuus)*

Gender: Hot

Planet: Sun

Element: Fire

Part used: Seed

Basic powers: Protection, fertility

Specific uses: The flowers growing in the garden
bring the blessings of the Sun. The seeds are
often eaten by women who wish to conceive.
This is done during the Waxing Moon.

Thistle *(Sonchus* spp.)

Gender: Hot

Planet: Mars

Element: Fire

Part used: The herb

Basic power: Protection

Specific uses: Throw onto a fire if you fear being
struck by lightning during a storm. Grow in the

garden to ward off thieves. A bowl of thistles in a room strengthens and energizes those within it, so they are often used in sickrooms or in places where people are recuperating.

Thyme *(Thymus vulgaris)*

Folk names: Garden thyme, common thyme

Gender: Cold

Planet: Venus

Element: Air

Part used: The herb

Basic powers: Clairvoyance, purification

Specific uses: Burn as incense to purge and fumigate magical rooms. Take a magical cleansing bath in the spring of thyme and marjoram. A pillow stuffed with thyme cures nightmares. Crush a handful of the fresh herb and inhale. You will at once be refreshed and renewed. Wear a sprig of the herb to funerals to protect yourself from the negativity of the mourners.

Tobacco *(Nicotiana tabacum)*

Gender: Hot

Planet: Mars

Element: Fire

Part used: Leaves

Basic power: Exorcism

Specific uses: Used by modern-day magicians as a replacement for sulphur, it is burned on charcoal to remove negativity. Throw tobacco into a river at the start of a journey on a boat. Tobacco smoke is sometimes used to cure illnesses by blowing the smoke on the diseased part of the body.

Tonka Beans *(Coumarouna odorata* or *Dipteryx odorata)*

Folk names: Tonqua, tonqua bean, tonquin bean, coumara nut

Gender: Cold

Planet: Venus

Element: Water

Part used: The bean

Basic power: Love

Specific use: Carry the bean in love sachets to attract love.

Valerian *(Valeriana officinalis)*

Folk names: Phu, all heal, amatilla, set well, capon's tailor, garden heliotrope, vandal root, fragrant valerian, St. George's herb, setuale, setwell, cat's valerian, English valerian

Gender: Cold

Planet: Mercury

Element: Water

Part used: The herb, root

Basic powers: Love, harmony

Specific uses: Use the fresh herb in spells of love, also to get fighting couples together. Used in the purification bath sachet.

Vanilla *(Vanilla aromatica* or *V. planifolia)*

Gender: Hot

Planet: Jupiter

Element: Fire

Part used: The bean

Basic power: Love

Specific uses: Though this herb is most often used in oil form, the whole bean is sometimes added to love charms or carried on the body to make one attractive and ready for an evening of loving. A vitalizing herb, used by some for get up and go!

Vervain *(Verbana officinalis)*

Folk names: Juno's tears, herb of grace, pigeon's grass, enchanter's plant, simpler's joy, holy herb, pigeonwood, herb of the cross, verbena, herb of enchantment, vervan, van-van, van van

Gender: Cold

Planet: Venus

Element: Water

Associated deities: Mars, Venus, Aradia, Cerridwen, Isis, Jupiter, Thor

Part used: The herb

Basic powers: Love, purification, protection

Specific uses: Magical cleansing baths, purification incenses, and personal safety amulets. Best gathered at Midsummer. Hang up on the bed to keep you free of nightmares. Helps soldiers escape their enemies. Bury in your fields to make the crops bountiful and profitable. Amulets are sometimes given to babies, for it is said to make its bearer a quick learner. Used in many love and protection sachets. Burn pure verain (or mix with equal parts of frankincense) for a fantastic purification in-cense. Use to attract wealth.

Violet *(Viola tricolor)*

Folk names: Blue violet, sweet violet

Gender: Cold

Planet: Venus

Element: Water

Associated deity: Venus

Part used: Flowers

Basic power: Love

Specific uses: Mix with lavender to make a powerful love sachet. A violet chaplet cures headaches. Carrying the flowers will bring a change of luck and fortune. Associated with sunset and twilight, so have on the altar if doing magic at these times.

Walnut *(Juglans regia)*

Folk names: Tree of evil, English walnut, Persian walnut, Caucasian walnut

Gender: Hot

Planet: Sun

Element: Fire

Part used: The nut

Basic powers: Fertility, healing

Specific uses: Carry the nut in its shell to promote
fertility, to strengthen the heart, or to ward off
rheumatism. Witches used to dance beneath
walnut trees in their rites, although this has
fallen into disuse. Because of the Witches' activ-
ities under the walnut trees, folk people began
viewing them with suspicion, hence its old folk
name, *Tree of Evil.* To find out if a person is a
Witch, drop a walnut on the lap of the sus-
pected party. If he or she is a Witch, they will
be unable to rise from the chair. This was one of
the methods of testiing Witch-es during the
Persecution. Eat walnuts to cure madness.

Willow *(Salix alba)*

Folk names: Tree of enchantment, Witches' aspirin, white willow, withe, withy, salicyn willow, osier, sough tree, saille

Gender: Cold

Planet: Moon

Element: Water

Associated deities: Artemis, Ceres, Hecate, Persephone, Circe, Hera, Mercury, Belili, Belinus

Part used: Branches

Basic powers: Healing, wishes

Specific uses: A wand made of willow is used in
healing rituals. The willow is used as the binding

208 ◄§ Witch's Herbal

on the Witch's broom. Called Tree of Enchantment in the language of the Witches, it is most often used to bring the blessings of the Moon into one's life. Plant a willow in the garden, preferably by a natural spring or river. It will guard your home admirably. The binding of the Witches' broom is often made of soft, pliant willow branches. Bear a sprig of this plant and you will be free from the fear of death. Tie a knot in a willow branch to serve as a physical representation of your intent for a spell. When the wish has been granted, untie the knot and then use again for a new spell.

Woodruff *(Asperula odorata)*

Folk names: Sweet woodruff, master of the woods, woodrove, wuderove, woodruffe, wuderofe, herb walter

Gender: Hot

Planet: Mars

Element: Fire

Part used: The herb

Basic power: Purification

Specific uses: An herb of the spring, used to clear away the closeness and drab atmosphere of the winter months. Carry when wishing to turn over a new leaf, or to change your outlook in life, especially in the spring. Added to the May wine, the traditional Witches' drink of their religious festival of Beltane. Brings victory to those who carry it.

Wormwood *(Artemisia absinthium)*

Folk names: Old woman, absinthe, absinth, crown for a king

Gender: Hot

Planet: Mars

Element: Air

Associated deities: Diana, Iris

Part used: The herb

Basic powers: Clairvoyance. protection

Specific uses: Once burned in all incenses designed to raise spirits, now used in clairvoyance and divinatory incenses (especially in combination with mugwort) as well as in exorcism and protection blends. Throw onto fires on Samhain (Halloween) to gain protection from the spirits roaming the night. Burn while using a pendulum. Fumigate to raise spirits, if you must.

Yarrow *(Achillea millefolium)*

Folk names: Seven years' love, sanguinary, old man's mustard, military herb, old man's pepper, soldier's woundwort, knight's milfoil, nosebleed, thousand seal, hundred-leaved grass, millefolium, milfoil, arrow root, eerie, ladies' mantle, knyghten, wound wort, stanch weed, field hops, tansy, gearwe, noble yarrow, yarroway, devil's bit, devil's plaything, achillea, snake's grass, death flower, stanch griss

Gender: Cold

Planet: Venus

Element: Water

Part used: Flowers

Basic powers: Love, clairvoyance, exorcism

Specific uses: Yarrow is used in love sachets and marriage charms, as it has the power to keep a couple together happily for seven years. Worn as an amulet, it wards off negativity. The tea drunk prior to divination will enhance one's powers of perception. Held in the hand, it stops all fear. It is sometimes added to exorcism incenses. The beautiful flowers are a welcome addition to any magical altar, as the yarrow is one of the Witch's favorite herbs.

PART THREE

The Magic Garden

© Robin Wood 1986

14

Your Herbal Garden

E very Witch worthy of her craft has an herb garden. Though simple in design, the Witches' garden contains a wealth of magical materials from which she concocts her sachets, incenses, aromatic oils, and charm bags.

A Witch knows simple gardening rules, tips on treating destructive pests, and general Earth wisdom. Much of what she knows is laid out in orderly fashion in this special section so that anyone, Witch or non-Witch, can grow herbs according to the old magical methods.

For those who cannot plant a garden, instructions for magical window- and indoor-gardening are included.

Selection of the Plants

Choose the herbs for your garden carefully. Decide your main sphere of interest. Do you intend to specialize your magical acts, or indulge in all areas of herbal magic? Are you limited strictly to the small herbs and flowers, or are trees to be included as well?

Answering these questions will basically answer the first question any would-be magical gardener has when planting a garden: what should I grow? Here are some lists of herbs suggested for various types of magic gardens. These are strictly suggestions, however; your own preferences and needs may vary.

Garden of love: Roses (the old varieties are much more suited to magic than the new), violets, vervain. yarrow, lavender, rosemary, basil, lemon balm, and lovage.

Healing garden: (By magical means, not medicinal) Peppermint, garlic, onion, carnation, rosemary, sage, rue, thistles, and wood sorrel.

Divination garden: Mugwort, yarrow, borage, cinquefoil, wormwood, anise, lavender.

General purpose garden: Rosemary, lavender, yarrow, vervain, hyssop, rue, carnation, mugwort, cinque foil, etc.

Use these lists as guides in drawing up a suitable group of plants for your garden.

Some Witches and magicians choose a selection of traditional plants such as the mandrake, henbane, periwinkle, foxglove, and nightshade without intending to ever put any of these herbs to use.

Whatever you decide, be sure you are satisfied with the final roster. Write the names of all the herbs you wish to grow and keep this by your side as you read the following pages, visualizing how each will fit into your garden.

Check your local nurseries and garden shops for seeds and live herbs. If none are available, write to the suppliers listed in appendix 3 for their catalogs.

Laying Out the Garden

Magic gardens are rarely formal affairs, laid out in intricate knot or maze patterns. Most are fairly organized plots arranged in a circular shape, the circle being the ancient symbol of fertility, reincarnation, and eternity. Some ambitious Witches fashion their gardens to resemble stars, suns, and cresent moons. The basic equipment needed here is a vivid imagination and a large supply of flat rocks, which are used to mark out the borders. With this type of garden, the idea is not merely to please the human eye, but also those forces that watch over us.

When you have decided on a pattern, or none at all, get a good book on herb gardening. Check the average heights of the herbs you wish to grow, and also any specific needs, such as shade, half-sun, full sunlight. Try to position herbs of like heights next to each other. Make a rough sketch of the area you have to garden and pencil in herbs as you decide on positioning.

There are traditional guidelines to follow here. Basil does not grow next to any other plant, so it is usually grown in a pot near the house. Sage and rue grow well together, as do coriander and dill. Mint and parsley dislike each other's company.

If you are going to plant trees, set the cypress to the north, elder to the east, bay laurel to the south, and willow to the west of the garden. If you must have a yew tree plant it in the southwest corner of the property. A maple or apple planted near the house is beneficial. But make sure that these trees will not shade the garden, for many herbs crave full, direct sunlight.

When the garden plan is firmly in mind, and on paper, collect the seeds and plants. Before they can be planted, the ground must be prepared.

Preparing the Land

Find a suitable plot of land, preferably on your own property, and where passersby will not disturb your plants. In spring, or when danger of frost has passed, take a handful of mistletoe and grind in the mortar three days after the New Moon. Sprinkle over the land. Work the soil well with a spade and trowel until it is light and moist. If the ground is too heavy, add a little mulch; if too sandy, add humus. Most herbs do not require perfect growing conditions but will produce more healthy growth if some care is given to the soil.

The basic shape of the garden, as stated earlier, is often circular. Lay a long string or light rope in the garden area in a circle, making its circumference as large as the space will allow. Be sure the ends of the rope are joined together with a good knot. If more than one piece of rope is required all connections should be thoroughly knotted.

Next, determine the four directions in your garden with a compass. Place stones outside the rope to mark these spots for later reference. The north stone should be clearly distinguished from the others.

Upon nightfall, build a small fire or set several lanterns around the area for illumination, if necessary.

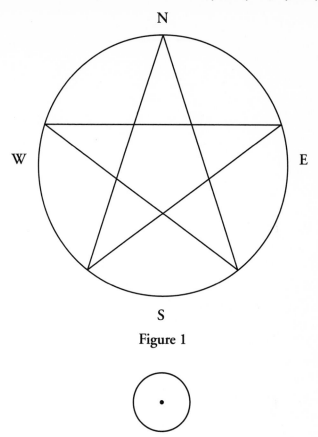

N

W   E

S

Figure 1

Figure 2

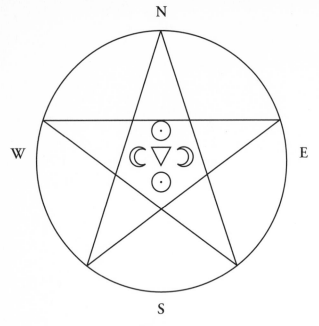

Figure 3

Starting in the north, plant a candle in the earth near the rope but outside the circle, light it, and then move clockwise following the same procedure at the east, south, and west points. If the night is windy, bring along four lanterns or clear-glass jars. If using the jars, pour a bit of melted wax inside each jar and fasten the candles within. Place these at the points as directed above.

Now, stand in the center of the circle and face north, holding your magic knife. Lift your arms skyward and say (or shout, if the wind is particularly rough):

I call upon the powers of the north to
bless and protect this garden.

Repeat to the east, south, and west, substituting the appropriate direction in the invocation.

Finished, turn to face north again. The star (Figure 1, page 217) should be drawn so that the uppermost point touches the north-facing candle, and the others, evenly spaced around the circle, touch the rope.

Now, while kneeling in the southern section of the pentagram, trace the symbols in Figure 2 (page 217) with the point of your knife in the earth.

Make sure the top symbol is touching the top of the crossing line of the pentagram, so that your garden looks like Figure 3 (page 218).

Now sit quietly, counting ninety heartbeats. Then, if you are satisfied that the garden is magically protected, blow the candles out, starting at the north point. If you have used glass jars, tip each one to allow the wind to quench the flames. Gently cut a branch from a birch mountain ash, or willow, or any nearby tree if these are unavailable. (If there are no trees, use the household broom, or one bought specifically for this purpose, which is better.)

As you gently cut with your magic knife, tell the tree the need you have for the branch, and afterward as payment, leave something buried in the ground beneath it.

Holding the branch in your strong hand, stand north outside the circle and begin to brush away the symbols that you have drawn. Walk in a clockwise direction and continue to brush until the ground is clear.

Gather up the rope and candles and store them away in a safe place. Quench any illumination fires or lanterns you may have lit.

The next morning, just as the Sun rises, search the ground for symbols. Sometimes specific patterns or symbols will appear on the ground, although it was swept clean the night before. Bird feathers are also often found. If dew has covered the ground with a carpet of liquid blessings, allow it to dry. Gather up any feathers and record magical symbols, for these are links between your garden and the silent forces of nature.

Pour one quart pure, unfiltered apple cider (fermented, if possible) into an earthenware vessel and stand in the middle of the garden. With your strong hand, sprinkle the cider round the garden, turning on the midpoint like an axle. When the cider is gone, leave the garden and let it soak up the liquid. The cider represents blood; it awakens and renews the energies residing in the earth and prepares it for the coming planting.

Leave the garden untouched for three days. Make sure that no person or animal walks on it. Animals are often hard to keep away, for they are naturally curious about the pleasing vibrations emanating from the blessed spot.

On the fourth day, rise before the Sun. The time for planting has come.

The Planting

Planting is guided by the Moon, as is much of a Witch's life. Herbs that contain their usefulness in seeds, leaves, and flowers are planted during the Waxing Moon. Root crops, such as angelica, mandrake, and peony, should be planted while the Moon is on the wane during the third or last quarter.

Some Witches who follow the movement of the Moon through the zodiac will plant herbs only during the moist and fertile signs. These best times to plant are while the Moon is in Cancer, Scorpio, Pisces, Taurus, and Capricorn.

Trees, as they are perennials and must develop strong roots to remain alive, are planted during the Waning Moon, and best of all after the last quarter but before the New Moon.

Flowers, or those herbs specifically valued for their blossoms, such as the lavender and carnation, should be planted while the Moon is in her increase (the first quarter is preferred) and in the sign of Libra for delicious fragrance and beauty. If abundance is more the concern, then plant flowers while the Moon is in Cancer, Scorpio, or Pisces.

To find the phases of the Moon and its daily astrological sign, consult an astrological almanac.

If you have followed the above procedures, the day of planting should fall upon the day after the first quarter begins. This means that one week remains to finish the above-ground crops.

Naturally, if you are planting by the Moon signs, adjust the following procedures accordingly, to correspond with the correct phase of the Moon and the desired sign.

Gather together the seed packets and/or live seed-lings. Place them just as they are in the center of the garden, and then go out and buy or make wooden stakes one inch wide and nine inches long. With black waterproof ink write the name of each herb on the stake on both sides. Then, taking up the seeds, plant them according to the directions on the package, following the design you previously laid out. As you sow each herb, place the stake that bears its name facing its section. Continue until planting is finished. (Remember, plant only the above-ground crops; roots are planted later.)

Plant any seedlings or plants next, and then with rain water or spring water gently sprinkle the garden. As you spread the water talk to your herbs, use your active imagination to visualize the garden not as a wet patch of earth, but as the beautiful growing ground it will soon be.

With care, time, and magic, your garden will blossom into life. Be careful that the seedlings are never allowed to go dry and be sure to plant only when any danger of frost is passed if you live in a cold climate. Thin the seedlings if they do not thin themselves. When your herbs have grown to a healthy size and are bushy and vibrant, then, and only then, begin to harvest them, following the directions given in that section of this book.

Protecting the Garden

The initial protection ritual given for the garden may be supplemented from time to time using any of the following methods.

One of the oldest protections is to plant three red flowers, such as geraniums, nasturtiums, and red roses, in the garden. These will serve to keep unwanted visitors away from your land.

To protect the garden from storms and hail, be sure to plant vervain somewhere near it or within the garden itself. A bay laurel tree helps protect it from lightning as well.

Trees may be protected with the quaint Celtic custom of tying red ribbons around the trunk while saying an appropriate rune, such as the following:

Elder tree,
secure thou will be.

or,

Sacred oak tree, hear my cry:
for your protection this I tie.

Be sure to replace the ribbons at regular intervals on the Full Moon. This same ritual can be done to some of the more sturdy herbs as well.

Destructive insects are an age-old problem to both Witch and normal gardener alike. To most effectively rid your garden of these, carry out any of the following procedures while the Waning Moon is in one of the barren signs, such as Leo, Virgo, Aries, Aquarius, or Gemini.

Sprinkle ground cayenne pepper around the base of each afflicted plant (good for crawling pests), or spray them with a solution made of one cup water to one-quarter cup onion juice (liquified in a blender) to one tablespoon liquid soap, such as a biodegradable dish-washing detergent. Mix this well and spray it on the plants. If any of the solution gets on the ground, flush the area well with water. After a few days, wipe the leaves clean of the soap and insects, and then spray with fresh, clean water. If problems persist, try nature's way. Many nurseries sell live ladybugs by the thousands. They are inexpensive and can effectively clear a garden of smaller insects quite fast. Praying mantis are also available in many locations.

Planting marigolds and rue among the other plants is another popular method of controlling the pests. Many insects hate the odors of these herbs.

Failing everything else, buy one of those organic plant sprays and use it according to instructions.

One old method of dealing with those animals who delight in munching on magical herbs is to make a straw image of the offending creatures. Bury it in the garden in one of the barren Moon signs and you should have no more problems.

Finally, during winter months if you live in an area that receives freezing temperatures and/or snow, cover your garden with a thick mulch. Leave this on until spring has definitely arrived, and danger of frost is passed.

Magical Gardening

Witches have been growing herbs for centuries, so they have amassed a wealth of procedures for effective magical gardening. Sometimes these make more sense than a pile of gardening books. (Recommended herbal gardening books, however, are listed in the bibliography.)

When the seedlings are well established, other uninvited plants will probably poke through the ground. Let some of these grow provided that they do not crowd your herbs, for many will be useful in magic. Typically, non-Witch gardeners often destroy such plants, little realizing their powers.

There are specific pruning rules. All pruning should be carried out in the decrease of the Moon. Hedges (such as the hawthorn, which at one time every Witch had in her garden) should always be trimmed from east to west, which follows the course of the Sun. Prune trees in a clockwise direction as you walk around them.

Thistles can be a bit of a bother in the garden. If you cut them after Midsummer, two will grow for every one you cut. Be sure to cut them well before June 21 unless you want a lot of thistles.

You may wish to share your herbs with friends. That is fine, but even here there are strict rules. Never give a part of a plant to a friend. If the person asks you for a sprig of, say, fresh rosemary, change the subject and walk away. They must steal a bit for themselves. If this procedure is followed, the plant will stay healthy and flourish.

Once a month, after the herbs are fully grown, on the night of the Full Moon, if possible, walk out to the garden and draw a circle in the dirt around each plant, using your knife. Make sure that the ends of the circle meet. Draw clockwise. This helps to seal the powers inside the leaves and roots.

Then, too, go out at night when the herbs are rejuvenating and basking in the Moon's light and talk to them. Never neglect this, for it creates a bond between you, a merging of your energy and the plant's energy. If your neighbors overhear your nocturnal conversations, do not worry. Many people talk to their plants today and many psychiatrists believe that it is excellent therapy.

One last note: to ensure that the destructive insect population is kept down, have a large frog or toad in the garden. Dub it with a good toadish name, like Gick or Trog, and talk to it whenever you walk in the garden. Give it a mate, and plenty of water, and it should stay.

Indoor Gardening

For those who cannot afford, or do not have room for outdoor gardening, consider indoor gardening. Be sure to plant the seeds in the proper phases of the Moon in the pots or window-boxes and follow to whatever lengths possible the above directions.

Situate these plants where they will receive some sunshine. Glazed terra-cotta pots work best. Three hours after watering a plant in an unglazed pot the earth will be dry inside. Plastic pots are not favored.

Take the plants outside once a week and spray with a light mist of water. Also allow them to receive direct sunlight on a regular basis, if they need sunshine, as window glass screens out some of the Sun's vital energies.

The artificial grow-lights now in use by some gardeners are fine but not for magical herbs! Even though the garden has been moved indoors, many of the old procedures can be followed.

A magic garden, to be just that, is more than a collection of plants with mysterious and fabled pasts. It is a place where energy meets energy, where the old forgotten magic of the earth lies in waiting within the enchanting elecampane or the sacred vervain. It is a glade where birds sing and dew collects to form moon-pools in tightly curled leaves and scented flowers.

It is a place where the wise, if they kneel upon the earth and listen carefully, can hear the heartbeat of nature murmuring softly in a single leaf of a single stalk of one of the billion plants nurtured by our blessed planet.

Witches respect all forms of life, including plants. Fortunately, herbs are hopelessly self-sacrificing. They were scattered on our planet to nourish and aid us in our practice of magic.

Never fail to ask permission of any plant from which you wish to pluck a leaf or flower, or to leave something beside it as payment for the part taken.

The garden path can lead to a strange world paved with spells and enchantments. If you fashion such a wonder, tread its paths lightly, for soon the roar of civilization may become unappealing, and like the Witch, you may find your greatest joy in mixing up love charms and healing philters while the wind laughs and whispers through the trees.

Appendices

Appendix 1

The Magical Names of Herbs, Flowers, Trees, and Roots

When the old recipes began to be recorded, many early herbalists, Witches, magicians, and occultists wished to keep secret the most powerful of the old magic. So they used magical names and symbolism and even added fanciful ingredients to the formulae.

Even today, scholars look over old manuscripts. shake their heads, and wonder why old occultists used such horrifying ingredients as *the ear of a Jew, bloody fingers, dove's feet, bat's wings,* and so on.

The often-quoted illustration from Shakespeare's *Macbeth* serves as a useful example of this practice. Every ingredient he lists as being in the Witches' pot (fillet of a fenny snake / in the cauldron boil and bake: / eye of newt, and toe of frog, / Wool of bat, and tongue of dog, / adder's fork, and blind-worm's sting / Lizard's leg, and howlet's wing, / etc.) refers to a plant and not to the gruesome substance popularly thought.

The list of such names is quite long and varied, but a few examples can be given here. *Bloody fingers* refers to foxglove. *Tongue of dog* is simply hound's tongue, a common herb. *Blood* is the sap from an elder tree. *Eyes* mean any one of a group of plants resembling the eye, as the aster, daisy, camomile, or perhaps even eyebright. *Crow's foot, dog's tooth, horse-tongue,* and *Jew's ear* are all magical and dialectical names for herbs and plants.

Then, too, many plants were given folk names that reveal their uses in magic or the superstitions surrounding them. This is especially common in the British Isles, where one plant can be known by as many as two dozen distinct names.

Finally, there are a whole bookful of plants with appelations such as *our ladies fingers* or *old man's oatmeal.* These are plants originally dedicated to the pagan goddesses and gods of the common folk and after the introduction of Christianity were assigned new roles as representative of the Virgin Mary and the Devil, respectively.

Following is a list of some magical names of herbs, along with their more common ones. Knowing these names may not give you additional power, but reading them is like taking a walk through a Witch's garden, and to the keen eye the old names reveal magical uses and a good deal of folklore.

Candlemas maiden: Snowdrop

Candlewick plant: Mullein

Crown for a king: Wormwood

Dew of the sea: Rosemary

Dragonwort: Bistort

Dwale: Deadly nightshade

Earth smoke: Fumitory

Elfwort: Elecampane

Enchanter's plant: Vervain

Eye of the star: Horehound

Five finger grass: Cinquefoil

Golden star: Avens

Honey lotus: Melilot

Joy of the mountain: Marjoram

Little dragon: Tarragon

Love-in-idleness: Pansy

Love parsley: Lovage

Loveroot: Orris

Maiden's ruin/Lad's love: Southernwood

Master of the woods: Woodruff

Masterwort: Angelica

May lily: Lily of the valley

Mistress of the night: Tuberose

Password: Primrose

Queen of the meadow: Meadowsweet

Ram's head: American valerian

Seven years' love: Yarrow

Sleep wort: Lettuce

Sorcerer's violet: Periwinkle

Starflower: Borage

Star of the earth: Avens

Starweed: Chickweed

Starwort: Aster

Thousand seal: Yarrow

Thunder plant: Houseleek

Unicorn horn: True unicorn root

Wax dolls: Fumitory

Witches aspirin: White willow bark

Witches bells: Foxglove

Witch grass: Dog grass

Witch herb: Mugwort

Witchwood: Rowan

Witches briar: Brier hip

Appendix 2

Baneful Herbs and Flying Ointments

Witches classify *baneful* herbs as those that produce death. Most herbalists list them as poisons, and warn others not to use them.

But the Witches once used them in their magical arts. Many of the fears that surround these plants are directly related to their magical powers. They are not to be played with precisely because they are powerful.

No one should let a child play with a razor-sharp knife. Similarly, none but the most experienced and knowledgeable Witches should use these herbs. They are not innocuous *highs* or instruments of escape from reality. They represent the dark side of Mother Nature, the realm of sleep, and coma, and death, and anyone not sufficiently prepared and tutored who uses them will be subject to her greatest wrath.

I assure you that I am not overdramatizing. Death stalks those who use such methods. The Witch, after years of experience and training, can be fairly sure of herself and her ritualistic use of baneful herbs. Others cannot.

This information is included because of its historical value, and a book on magical herbalism would not be complete without a look at the *darker* side of the art. No recommendations for these uses are made. Even the most harmless of them can cause severe effects in some individuals.

Belladonna *(Atropa belladonna)*

Once used to induce astral projection and visions, belladonna is one of the herbs nearly everybody associates with Witchcraft and magic. One of the most grisly uses the Witches made of it was to deaden pain during the Persecution. The crowds that pressed up against condemned Witches as they were being led to the pyre or scaffold nearly always contained a few other Witches. One of these would try to slip a bit of this herb to the Witch. She then swallowed it and the herb helped her drowse her way to the other world. The old Witches called it *dwale* or *banewort*, and it was a common ingredient in flying ointments. Witches also used it to deaden the pain of childbirth. It was always picked on May Eve and it is sacred to Hecate.

The priestesses in ancient Greece used this herb for divinatory practices, as did early Witches. It is thought to have been introduced into Europe in the fifteenth or sixteenth century, but was in use in the Americas for centuries prior to that time.

Southwestern Amerindian lore is filled with references to jimsonweed, as it is also known. They used it much like the old Witches did, for causing visions and to counteract spells and hexes. The plant is so virulently poisonous that the touch of some species is enough to cause dermatitis.

Fly Agaric *(Amanita muscaria)*

The magic mushroom has been used in secret rituals all over the world, and the Witches were no exception. This fungus was brewed into a tea and drunk directly before admission rituals to the Craft. It was also drunk to aid clairvoyance. Some Witches kept a fly agaric on their altars.

Hellebore *(Helleborus niger)*

Both the black and green varieties of hellebore were used in incenses to cause frenzy. Witches did not use such incenses but mischievous sorcerers and magicians—or herbalists who decided to pay back a few of the priests for their continual harassment—might introduce a bit of this herb into the censers during the church ceremonies and stand outside, waiting for the congregation to turn violent and unruly. This was a typical magical joke of several centuries ago.

Hellebore was also used in the flying ointments, those made to induce astral projection. The root of black hellebore, when powdered and scattered on the ground, was thought to make one invisible.

It was also used in exorcism and countermagic incenses, and the fresh herb was pressed against the forehead to stop a headache. Grecian Witches faced east and cursed while cutting it.

238 ◦§ Appendix 2

Hemlock *(Conium maculatum)*

Once used in spells to destroy sexual drives and in suicide drinks (i.e. Socrates), hemlock is still virulently poisonous and is dedicated to Hecate. It was used in flying ointments.

Hemp *(Gannihis sativa)*

Hemp, the old Witches' name for marijuana, shows up in a lot of old rituals, spells, and recipes, usually of the *love* or *divination* type. One old instruction called for the Witch to burn hemp and mugwort while gazing into a crystal ball. No doubt such recipes would be effective, for marijuana has long been celebrated as a relaxant that allows the mind to slip away from everyday tensions and enter a kind of limbo between normal waking consciousness and sleep. This is very near the state many Witches need to attain prior to achieving clairvoyance.

Hemp also figures into many love spells. It was once administered in love potions, because it had the ability to relax the defenses, and makes a person more susceptible to another's suggestions and control.

Marijuana is probably the most talked-about herb of this century. Witches have known its powers and weaknesses for many centuries. Some Witches make use of it regularly in their rites, but others will not even be in the same room with the herb. Until the 1930s, when its cultivation, sale, and use was restricted by the federal government in this country, Witches used it with some regularity in their rites. (At least one sect of Witches is known to have included marijuana in the incense they burned during their religious and magical rites.) Though many Witches continue to use it, others have turned to different methods.

The biggest danger from marijuana is that it tends to take control of the user; one is compelled to use it more and more, and thusly, become dependent upon it. This is dangerous to the magician; you must be in firm control of your life. Drug addiction is a sign of weakness.

Witches who use marijuana control their usage and generally indulge only for magical reasons. It is included in many vision incense recipes.

Henbane *(Hyoscyarnus niger)*

This herb was used to call up evil entities, and to induce clairvoyance. It was also used in countermagic spells, and to attract the love of a woman.

The Flying Ointment

These, then, are the major baneful herbs that were used in magic. Others, among them foxglove, aconite, and water parsnip, were also used, to a lesser extent. Many of these were combined into a single, powerful concoction: the flying ointment.

The herbs were shredded and powdered, then steeped in hog's lard or some other fat. This ointment, when rubbed onto the body, quickened the heartbeat, increased the rate of respiration, and made the whole body turn red.

The Witches anointed themselves and then laid down, usually beside the hearth. They then flew through the air and met with other Witches, discussed their spells, and performed magical rituals.

It was important to keep the body of the Witch warm, and this was why he or she laid down by the fireplace. When the Witches told of these wonders to their torturers, the Christians believed that the physical body of the Witch flew through the air, and that it exited via the chimney that was right near where the Witch performed the anointing.

In fact, the Witches were experiencing astral projection. Their physical bodies lay inert, seemingly lifeless, while the Witch's full consciousness traveled at will. The drugs in the flying ointments allowed the Witch to attain this state simply by applying the ointment to the body.

The mad stories of orgies, devil worship, and so on were the product of the imaginations of overzealous Christians who desired to give more justification to their mass slaughter of innocent human beings. These things did not happen.

Most of the Witches did not believe that they flew through the air in the way the Christians thought that they did. There may have been a few who did. Witches simply accepted what older, more experienced Witches passed on to them. What mattered was that the ointment worked.

Over sixty formulae for flying ointments have survived. Most are bastardizations and simply variations on a theme. The real formulas always contained a fat, to facilitate application to the body, as well as three or more of the above-named herbs. Some Witches added soot (to represent the other realm that they visited while using the ointment) and a few drops of their own blood (to make the ointment uniquely personal).

Other herbs that were often included are basil, cinque-foil, sunflower seeds, parsley, and sweet flag. These were used for their magical and symbolic powers, and not for any direct physical affect.

These ointments have been handed down to present-day Witches as Sabbat oils. These are worn when performing magical rites, especially when two or more Witches gather together to perform their mystic religious rituals.

Such oils are fine for general magical use as well. A few are given in chapter 10 under *Anointing Oils*.

©Robin Wood 1986

Appendix 3

Sources for Herbs and Oils

There are many mail-order companies that supply herbs. However, this appendix lists only a few of those known to be reliable and that are well-established.

Aphrodisia
264 Bleecker Street
New York, NY 10014
212-989-6440
www.aphrodisiaproducts.com
Dried herbs, plus a large selection of natural and compounded oils, self-lighting charcoal, books, exotic cooking specialities. Send a postcard for a current catalog.

Burgess Seed & Plant Co.
905 Four Seasons Road
Bloomington, IL 61701
309-663-9551
www.eburgess.com
Herb seeds and plants.

244 ~§ Appendix 3

Henry Field's Seed and Nursery Co.
415 North Burnett
Shenandoah, IA 51602
605-665-9391
Herb seeds and plants.

Indiana Botanic Gardens
3401 West 37th Ave.
Hobart, IN 46342
219-947-4040
info@botanichealth.com
Exotic herbs and oils.

Nichols Garden Nursery
1190 N. E. Salem Road
Albany, OR 97321
541-928-9280
800-422-3985

George W. Park Seed Co.
Greenwood, SC 29647
800 845-3369
www.parkseed.com
Herb seeds, along with a wide variety of unusual seeds for
many kinds of plants. Also a wonderful color catalog.

Appendix 4

Herbal Redes

What can kill, can cure.

More in the garden grows
than the Witch knows.

Sell your coat, and buy betony.

No ear hath heard, no tongue can tell,
the virture of the pimpernel.

Treoil, vervain, St. John's wort, dill,
hinder Witches of all their will.

Where rosemary grows,
the missus is master.

Faerie-folks,
are in old oaks.

Sow fennel,
sow sorrow.

Only the wicked grow parsley.

Plant your sage and rue together,
the sage will grow in any weather.

Snakes will not go
where geraniums grow.

Where the yarrow grows,
there is one who knows.

If ye would herbal magic make,
be sure the spell in rhyme be spake.

Woe to the lad
without a rowan tree god (amulet).

Rowan tree and red thread,
put the Witches to their speed.

Eat an apple going to bed,
make the doctor beg his bread.

The fair maid who, the first of May
goes to the fields at break of day,
and washes in dew from the hawthorn tree
will ever after handsome be.

Plant not a cypress vine,
unless it bring death to thine.

Beware the oak, it draws the stroke.
avoid the ash, it courts the flash.
Creep under the thorn,
it will save you from harm.

An apple a day
keeps the doctor away.

Flowers out of season,
sorrow without reason.

He would live for aye,
must eat sage in May.

One to rot, one to grow,
One for the pigeon and one for the crow.

St. John's wort and cyclamen
in your bed-chamber keep,
from evil spells and witcheries,
to guard you in your sleep.

I borage
give courage.

No mistletoe,
no luck.

Be silent as the sacred oak!

Bibliography

Early Sources

Apuleius. *Herbarium.*

Coles, William. *The Art of Simpling.* London: 1656. Reprinted St. Catherine's (Ontario, Canada): Provoker Press, 1968.

Culpeper, Nicholas. *The English Physician.* London: 1652. Reprinted London: Foulsham, N.D. as *Culpeper's Complete Herbal.*

Gerard, John. *The Herball, or Generall Historie of Plants.* London: 1597. Reprinted New York: Dover, 1975.

Goodyer, John, translator. *The Greek Herbal of Dioscorides.* 1655. Robert Gunther, editor, 1933. New York: Hafner, 1968.

Leaves from Gerard's Herbal. Arranged by Marcus Woodward. New York: Dover, 1969.

Pliny the Elder. *Natural History.*

The Powers of Plants

Bolton, Brett L. *The Secret Powers of Plants.* New York: Berkeley Medallion, 1974.

Tompkins, Peter, and Christopher Bird. *The Secret Life of Plants.* New York: Avon Books, 1974.

Whitman, John. *The Psychic Power of Plants.* London: Star Books, 1974.

Herb Lore and Legend

Budge, E. A. Wallis. *Herb Doctors and Physicians in the Ancient World: The Divine Origin of the Craft of the Herbalist.* Chicago: Ares Publishers, 1978.

Emboden, William A. *Bizarre Plants: Magical, Monstrous, Mythical.* New York: Macmillan, 1974.

Grigson, Geoffrey. *A Herbal of all Sorts.* New York: Macmillan, 1959.

Kamm, Minnie Watson. *Old-Time Herbs for Northern Gardeners.* Boston: Little, Brown and Co., 1938.

Leek, Sybil. *Sybil Leek's Book of Herbs.* New York: Thomas Nelson, 1973.

Porteous, Alexander. *Forest Folklore, Mythology & Romance.* London: George Allen & Unwin Ltd., 1928. Reprinted Detroit: Singing Tree Press, 1968.

Thistleton-Dyer, T. F. *The Folklore of Plants.* Detroit: Singing Tree Press, 1968.

Medicinal Use of Herbs

Lust, John. *The Herb Book.* New York: Bantam, 1974.

Rose, Jeanne. *Herbs and Things: Jeanne Rose's Herbal.* New York: Grosset & Dunlap, 1972.

Royal, Penny C. *Herbally Yours.* Provo, Utah: Bi-World Publishers, 1976.

Grimoires and Spellbooks

Barrett, Francis. *The Magus, or Celestial Intelligencer.* London, 1801. Reprinted New Hyde Park, New York: University Books, 1967.

Best, Michael, and Frank H. Brightman, editors. *The Book of Albertus Magnus of the Vertues of Herbs, Stones, and Certain Beasts, also A Book of the Marvels of the World.* Oxford: Oxford University Press, 1973.

Lady Sheba. *The Grimoire of Lady Sheba.* St. Paul: Llewellyn Publications, 1973.

Mathers, S. Liddell MacGregor, translator and editor. *The Key of Solomon.* New York: Weiser, 1972.

Shah, Sayed Idries. *The Secret Lore of Magic.* New York: The Citadel Press, 1970.

Worth, Valerie. *The Crone's Book of Words.* St. Paul: Llewellyn Publications, 1971.

Perfumes, Oils, and Incenses

Fettner, Ann Tucker. *Potpourri, Incense and Other Fragrant Concoctions.* New York: Workman Publishing Co., 1977.

Maple, Eric. *The Magic of Perfume.* New York: Weiser, 1973.

Thompson, C. J. S. *The Mystery and Lure of Perfume.* Philadelphia: J. B. Lippincott & Co., 1927.

Tisserand, Robert B. *The Art of Aromatherapy.* New York: Inner Traditions International Ltd., 1977.

Trueman, John. *The Romatic Story of Scent.* New York: Doubleday, 1975.

Growing Herbs

How To Grow Herbs. Menlo Park, Calif.: Sunset Books, 1972.

Huson, Paul. *Mastering Herbalism.* New York: Stein & Day, 1974.

Simmons, Adelma Grenier. *Herb Gardening in Five Seasons.* Princeton: D. Van Nostrand Co., 1964.

Moon Gardening and Planetary Hours

The Moon Sign Book. St. Paul: Llewellyn Publications. Published annually.

George, Llewellyn. *The Improved Perpetual Planetary Hour Book.* St. Paul: Llewellyn Publications, 1975.

Riotte, Louise. *Planetary Planting.* New York: Simon and Schuster, 1975.

Magic Gardens and Magical Gardening

Baker, Margaret. *Gardener's Magic & Folklore.* New York: Universe Books, 1978.

Boland, Bridget. *Gardener's Magic and Other Old Wive's Lore.* New York: Farrar, Straus & Giroux, 1977.

Jacob, Dorothy. *A Witch's Guide to Gardening.* New York: Taplinger, 1965.

Magic and Herbalism

Cunningham, Lady Sara. *The Magical Virtues of Candles, Herbs, Incense and Perfume.* Glendale, Calif.: Aleph Books, 1979.

Frazer, Sir James. *The Golden Bough.* New York: Macmillan, 1956.

Graves, Robert. *The White Goddess.* New York: Farrar, Straus & Giroux, 1973.

Leland, Charles Godfrey. *Etruscan Magic and Occult Remedies.* New Hyde Park, N. Y.: University Books, 1963.

Leyel, C. F. *The Magic of Herbs.* New York: Harcourt Brace, 1926.

Pepper, Elizabeth, and John Wilcox. *Witches All.* New York: Grosset & Dunlap, 1977.

Radford, E. and M. A. *Encyclopedia of Superstitions.* Edited and revised by Christina Hole. London: Hutchinson, 1961.

Randolph, Vance. *Ozark Supersitions.* New York: Columbia University Press, 1947.

Schmidt, Philip, S. J. *Supersition and Magic.* Westminster, Md.: The Newman Press, 1963.

Valiente, Doreen. *Natural Magic.* New York, St. Martin's Press, 1975.

Index

acacia, 60, 90, 107, 125, 136
accidents, 171
aconite, 239
acorn, 6, 53, 133, 182–184
Adonis, 137, 180, 192
Aesculapius, 142
agriculture, 21, 88
agrimony, 131
air, 8, 38, 63, 77–78, 87, 89–90,
    93–95, 99, 136, 138, 143,
    145, 148, 154, 158–159, 164,
    171–172, 175–178, 181,
    189–190, 196, 198, 200, 202,
    209, 239–240
air fluid condenser, 94–95
alcohol, 42, 44, 70–71, 93, 102
alder, 91
all-spice, 107
almond, 108, 129
altar, 16, 19, 23–25, 49, 51, 53, 55,
    60–61, 63, 72–73, 82, 104, 110,
    121, 149, 174, 177, 206, 210
ambergris, 61, 103
amulet, 39, 74–75, 109, 115,
    137–138, 141–142, 152, 178,
    191, 195, 199, 210, 247
anaphrodisiac, 39, 148, 173
anemone, 137

angelica, 50–51, 55, 91, 96, 137,
    221, 233
animals, 10, 78, 103, 132, 141, 179,
    220, 224
anise, 36, 60, 66, 90, 92, 108, 138,
    200, 214
anointing, 54–55, 96, 102–104,
    108, 111, 115, 240–241
    oils, 9, 11, 24, 26, 29, 60–61,
        74, 82, 88, 99–117, 143,
        166, 191, 198, 213, 241,
        243–244
aphrodisiac, 39, 106, 109–110, 116
Aphrodite, 156, 175, 180
Apollo, 139, 142, 165, 187
Apple, 6, 26, 44, 83–84, 91, 101,
    108, 133, 138–139, 147, 174,
    194, 216, 220, 247–249
    blossoms, 35, 49, 78, 84, 139,
        155, 185, 221
    cider, 44, 101, 139, 220
    cider vinegar, 44, 101
Aradia, 195, 205
Artemis, 164, 178, 180, 207
Arthur, King, 139
asafoetida, 50, 139
ash, 6, 26, 50, 91, 133, 140, 174,
    194, 219, 247

Ashtoreth, 156, 180
Astarte, 136, 180
aster, 83, 232, 234
astral projection, 236–237, 240
Athena, 139
athletics, 21, 89
Attis, 190
Avens, 50, 55, 132, 140, 233–234

Baal, 161
Bacchus, 170
bachelor's buttons, 82–83
balm of Gilead, 50, 83, 85, 90, 141
banishings, 3, 10, 20, 40, 55,
        71–72, 75–76, 88–89, 95,
        114–115, 119, 122, 125, 197
basil, 26, 50, 55–56, 83–85, 91,
        108, 141, 214–215, 241
Bast, 149
bath, 7, 26–27, 49, 54–55, 60, 65,
        72, 104, 108, 110, 114, 138,
        142, 157, 169, 172–173, 185,
        191, 193–194, 202, 204
    purification, 6–7, 26–27,
            54–56, 104, 108, 110,
            112, 121–122, 138–139,
            142–146, 151, 157–158,
            161, 169, 172–173, 180,
            184, 189–190, 193–196,
            198–199, 202, 204–205,
            208
bayberry, 180
bay laurel, 11, 50, 53, 56, 62, 91,
        126–127, 142, 215, 222
bean, 76, 151, 165, 203–204
belili, 207
belladonna, 236
belinus, 207
benzoin tincture, 44, 73, 101, 143
bergamot, 77, 83, 108
birch, 6, 140, 219
bistort, 90, 132, 144, 232
black, 10–11, 67, 154, 221, 237
blessings, 6, 10, 110, 123, 195, 201,
        208, 220
blue, 10, 72–74, 77–78, 159, 192, 206
borage, 35, 131, 214, 234, 249

Brazil nut, 182
breathing, 63
broom, 40, 90, 140, 144, 208, 219
brown, 10, 35, 37, 200
bryony, 145, 174
buildings, 22, 88
burdock, 91, 146
business, 88, 108, 112–113, 123, 143

cactus, 146–147
calamus, 125
camomile, 74, 91, 96, 147, 232
camphor, 91, 108, 147–148
candles, 9, 16, 24, 49, 55–56,
        60–61, 63–64, 72, 82, 95–96,
        104–105, 107–109, 121, 159,
        168, 179, 217, 219–220
caraway, 83, 148
cardea, 163
carnation, 72, 74–75, 91, 103, 106,
        109, 132, 149, 214, 221
cassia, 60, 150
cat, 149–150, 204
catnip, 82, 91, 149
cauldron, 62, 231
cayenne, 223
cedar, 26, 90, 124, 128, 190
celandine, 91, 150
celibacy, 21
censer, 10, 24, 40, 50, 55–56, 61,
        67, 73, 119–120
Ceres, 142, 191, 207
Cerridwen, 142, 170, 183, 205
Cernunnos, 183
chaplet, 40, 133, 181, 193, 206
charcoal blocks, 10, 67, 119–120
chastity, 146, 163, 172
chicory, 62, 85
childbirth, 89, 109, 111, 169, 236
cinnamon, 11, 61, 66, 74, 82, 91,
        106, 109, 123–127, 129, 143,
        150–151
cinquefoil, 62, 90, 109, 128, 151,
        214, 233, 241
Circe, 174, 207
circle, 33, 79, 127, 164, 215–217,
        219, 225

circle incense, 127
civet, 103
clairvoyance, 21, 40, 42, 59–60, 62,
    64–65, 72, 89, 108, 110, 136,
    142, 144, 151, 159, 165,
    167–168, 175–176, 178, 182,
    187, 192, 196, 200–202,
    209–210, 237–239
  brew, 62, 64, 159
clockwise, 7, 33, 41, 55, 104, 217,
    219, 225
clove, 55, 61–62, 74, 77, 91, 109,
    132, 153, 162
clover, 64, 131, 152–153
colds, 70, 78, 110, 139, 148, 159
coltsfoot, 82
comfrey, 90, 131, 154
communications, 21, 89
conceive, 132, 144, 174, 178,
    182–183, 201
consecrate, 6, 8, 40, 156, 161, 180
cooking, 21, 243
copper, 40, 85
coriander, 36, 83, 91, 109, 154, 215
costmary, 67
counterclockwise, 44, 55
courage, 21, 105, 112, 114, 179, 249
cradle, 53, 157
crocus, 133, 196
crystal ball, 44, 238
cucumber, 77, 84, 91, 96, 155
cumin, 83, 109, 161
Cupid, 192
curse, 41, 181
  to remove, 7, 36, 75, 155, 181,
    184, 191, 203
Cybele, 183, 190
cyclamen, 49–50, 57, 85, 92, 109,
    132, 155, 249
cypress, 90, 105, 109, 156, 215, 247

Dagda, 183
daisy, 232
damiana, 124
death, 22, 85, 109, 149, 156, 208,
    210, 235, 247

Demeter, 192
Diana, 121, 136, 139, 164, 178,
    195, 209
Dianus, 183
diaphragm, 63
dill, 36, 50, 56, 156–157, 188, 215,
    245
Dionysius, 139, 170, 190
disease, 20, 71, 76, 79, 132, 137,
    139, 162
divination, 21, 41, 59–68, 89, 108,
    178, 187, 210, 214, 238
dragon's blood, 49–50, 82–83, 128,
    157
dreams, 21, 29, 60, 64, 67, 111,
    125, 143, 165, 175, 191, 193
drowning, 140, 162
  to protection against, 140
drug addiction, 89, 95, 239
drugs, 70–71, 240
drunkeness, to prevent, 69, 77–78,
    132–133, 144, 149, 152, 162,
    178, 182, 187
drying, 31–38, 50
dwale, 232, 236

earth, 4, 7–8, 18, 20, 25, 32–35, 38,
    65, 75, 87–88, 90, 94, 96, 99,
    109, 115, 140, 144–145, 151,
    153, 156, 160, 164, 166–168,
    170, 174, 186–187, 190,
    197–198, 213, 217, 219–220,
    222, 226, 233–234
earth fluid condenser, 94
earth, herbs of, 31–32, 81, 87–97, 215
east, 4, 24, 95, 107, 143, 215, 217,
    219, 225, 237
East Wind, 107
Egypt, 116
elder, 6, 90, 157–158, 215, 223,
    232
elecampane, 83, 92, 226, 233
elements, 28, 79, 87–97, 152–153
employers, 21
enchant, 41, 104, 121
enfleurage, 100, 103

Eros, 192
eucalyptus, 11, 74, 78, 90, 110, 159
exorcism, 41, 54, 121–122, 138–139,
141–143, 161–162, 165, 181,
184, 187–188, 193, 195–197,
200, 203, 209–210, 237
eyebright, 74, 90, 159, 232
eyesight, 109
eyedropper, 102, 105

faeries, 133
family, 18, 21, 89
far memory, 111
feathers, 220
fennel, 26, 50, 56, 179, 246
fern, 50, 90, 160, 165
fertility, 6, 10, 20, 27, 84–85, 88,
144, 155–156, 163–164, 174,
180, 182–183, 190–192, 201,
206–207, 215
fir, 6
fire, 4–5, 8–9, 15, 26, 36–37, 39, 44,
62, 67, 87–89, 91, 93–95, 99,
114–115, 137, 139, 141–143,
146, 149–151, 153–154,
156–157, 160, 162–163, 165,
167, 169, 171, 175, 178–179,
181, 183–184, 187–188,
192–197, 199, 201–204, 206,
208, 217
fire, element of, 95, 99, 137, 139,
141–143, 146, 149–151,
153–154, 156–157, 160,
162–163, 165, 167, 169, 171,
175, 179, 181, 183–184,
187–188, 192–197, 199, 201,
203–204, 206, 208
fith-fath, 43, 114
flax, 50
fluid condenser, 41, 87–97, 93–96,
99
fluids, magical, 41, 87–97
fly agaric, 237
flying ointment, 239
foxglove, 179, 214, 232, 234, 239
fragrance of Venus oil, 106

frankincense, 7, 10–11, 19, 24–25,
50, 56, 66–67, 103, 110,
122–124, 127–128, 144, 160,
205
Freya, 192
Friday, 21, 82, 85, 104, 106, 113,
129
friendships, 21, 89
fumitory, 50, 233–234
funerals, 22, 202

galangal, 126
gallows, 132, 174
to avoid, 108, 131–132, 152
garden magic, 215
gardenia, 92, 105, 110, 161
gardening, magical, 214, 224
garden, indoor, 225–226
garlands, 77
garlic, 53, 55–57, 74, 76, 78, 91,
132, 162, 184, 194, 214
gathering, 31–38
gender of herbs, 135, 139–141,
144–146, 150–151, 154, 159,
167, 169, 172–174, 177–179,
181, 186–187, 189–190, 193,
195, 197, 200–202, 204–205,
208
geranium, pink, 10, 82–84, 104, 163
ghost, 131, 172
ginger, 110
gold, 93, 97, 108, 164, 175
gossip, 153
graveyard dust, 179
Greece, ancient 25, 236
green, 10–11, 14, 20, 27, 56, 75,
82–83, 85, 159, 166, 168,
182, 200, 237
Gwidion, 140

Halloween, 209
hallucinogen, 42
handfasting oil, 105
haggling, 3
happiness, 72, 108, 111, 176

harmony, 105, 108–109, 111–113, 204
Hathor, 174, 180
Hawaii, 132
hawthorn, 53, 92, 133, 163, 225, 247
hazel, 6, 26, 84, 90, 164, 182, 195
headaches, 70, 77, 206
healing, 6, 10, 21, 43, 69–79, 89, 95, 109–111, 114–116, 137, 139–140, 142–143, 151, 153–155, 159, 163, 165, 168, 172, 180, 182, 184, 189, 193–198, 200, 206–208, 214, 227
  incense, 10, 21, 24, 27, 40, 50, 55–56, 60–62, 64, 73, 82, 99, 109, 113, 119–129, 149, 151, 160–161, 194, 196, 201–202, 239
  incense oil, 60, 99, 129
health, 10, 20, 71–72, 76, 88–89, 109, 151, 196
heart, 8, 84–85, 104, 141, 186, 207
heart strength, 207
heather, 92, 132, 164
Hecate, 155, 162, 174, 207, 236, 238
heliotrope, 91, 110, 133, 165, 203
hellebore, 39, 237
hemlock, 51, 182, 238
hemp, 238
henbane, 39, 82–83, 92, 165, 214, 239
henna, 125
Hera, 139, 207
herb, 8, 10, 19, 29, 32–34, 37–39, 41–42, 45, 64, 66, 76–78, 81, 93, 99–100, 105, 120, 135–136, 139–142, 144–146, 149–155, 157, 159–160, 162, 165, 167–170, 172–174, 176–181, 186–190, 193, 195–197, 200–202, 204–205, 208–210, 213, 215, 221–222, 232, 234, 236–239, 243–244
Hercules, 139, 156, 183

Herne, 183
High John the Conqueror, 90, 166
Holda, 158
holly, 26, 91, 167, 170
honey, 35, 64, 126, 233
honeysuckle, 85, 90, 107, 110, 129, 167
hops, 92, 145, 168, 210
horehound, 50, 90, 168, 233
horus, 73, 168
hound's tongue, 232
hours, planetary, 22–23, 33, 97
house, 19, 25, 36, 52–56, 78, 95, 112–114, 122, 146, 156, 160, 163–164, 167, 170, 176–177, 183, 186, 189, 197, 199, 215–216
Hulda, 192
hunting, 21, 89
hyacinth, 92, 110, 169
Hypnos, 191
hypnosis, 13
hyssop, 26, 50–51, 56, 91, 110, 169, 214

identifying, 31–38
illness, 20, 72, 75–76, 88, 139, 190, 196
impotency cure, 157, 174, 184
imprisonment, 150
  to escape, 150
Improved Perpetual Planetary Hour Book, 23
incantations, 29
incense, 10, 21, 24, 27, 40, 50, 55–56, 60–62, 64, 73, 82, 99, 109, 113, 119–129, 149, 151, 160–161, 194, 196, 201–202, 239
inertia, 196
infusion, 27, 42, 44, 64, 87
intellectual, 13, 100, 141, 143, 193, 195
intent, 17, 19, 41, 84, 94–95, 120, 123, 208
intuition, 40, 136
iris, 185, 209

iron, 35
Ishtar, 136
Isis, 73, 165, 180, 192, 205
Italy, 53
ivy, 77, 92, 131, 170

Janus, 183
jasmine, 83–84, 90, 104–106, 110,
    170–171
jewelry, 29, 96, 122
jimsonweed, 236
jobs, 36, 88
juniper, 26, 49, 51, 55, 61, 91,
    124–125, 171, 190, 194
Jupiter, 21–23, 128, 138, 140, 143,
    151, 165, 167, 169–170, 177,
    179, 181, 183, 196, 200,
    204–205

knife magic, 3, 6–7, 24, 33–35,
    52–53, 94–95, 121, 184, 190,
    217, 219
knot, 52, 66, 208, 215–216
Krishna, 142
kyphi, 125

lanterns, 217, 220
laurel, 11, 40–41, 50, 53, 56, 62, 67,
    91, 126–127, 142, 215, 222
lavender, 26, 36, 74, 77, 82–83, 90,
    106–107, 111, 128, 131,
    171–172, 185, 206, 214, 221
legal matters, 21
lemon balm, 67, 83, 128, 151, 214
lemon grass, 111
lemon verbena, 90, 132, 172
lettuce, 92, 173, 234
lifeforce, 16, 20, 45
lightning, 143, 158, 194–195, 202,
    222
    protection against, 143, 195, 222
lilac, 100, 111
longevity, 183
lotus, 74, 111, 123, 233

lovage, 83, 92, 173, 214, 233
love, 6, 10, 14, 18, 20–21, 25, 27,
    34, 81–85, 89, 96, 104–105,
    107–110, 113, 116, 129,
    138–139, 141–142, 148,
    150–151, 154–155, 157–158,
    160–161, 163, 166, 169–177,
    180–182, 185–187, 192–193,
    196, 200, 203–206, 210, 214,
    227, 233, 238–239
love incense, 82, 129
love oil, 104–105, 109, 113
luck, 21, 39, 41, 53, 108, 164, 195,
    206, 249
lust, 21, 173, 185

mace, 126
madness, to cure, 207
madness, to prevent, 152
magic, 3, 6–10, 13–29, 31, 33–35,
    38–45, 50, 52–53, 63, 69–72,
    75–76, 81, 83–84, 87, 89, 91,
    93–95, 97, 99–100, 102, 109,
    112, 119–121, 123, 135, 140,
    145–147, 158, 160, 174,
    178–179, 181–182, 184,
    190–191, 194–195, 199, 206,
    211, 213–215, 217, 219, 222,
    224–227, 231–232, 236–237,
    239, 246
    basic principles, 14
    places for, 18
    religious, 3, 8, 18, 23–24, 109,
        112, 119
    times for, 15, 18–20, 22, 27–28,
        35, 70, 194, 222
magic room, 19, 25–27, 29, 72,
    145–146
magnetic oil, 108, 110, 112
magnolia, 111
mandrake, 53, 77, 83–84, 90, 133,
    140, 145, 174, 214, 221
manifestations, 42, 139, 141, 176
maple, 216
Marian, 180
marigold, 36, 91, 175

marriage charms, 96, 210

Mars, 21–22, 76, 128, 137, 140, 142, 145–146, 154, 157, 162–163, 167–168, 181, 184, 188, 190, 201–202, 205, 208–209

mastic, 61, 90, 125, 176

May apple, 174

May Day, 53, 152

May Eve, 236

meadowsweet, 83, 92, 176–177, 233

medicine, 21, 89

meditation, 22, 28, 60, 89, 107, 109, 111, 113, 124–125, 136, 147, 161

meditation incense, 124

melilot, 111, 233

melon, 97

mental powers, 10, 114, 126, 164

Mercury, 21–22, 128, 148, 152, 156, 158, 164, 168, 171, 174–175, 190, 204, 207

midnight, 20, 24

Midsummer, 144, 160, 172, 177, 197, 205, 225

military service, 131, 152

mimosa, 111

mint, 26, 67, 77, 82, 112, 166, 175–176, 187, 189, 200, 215

mistletoe, 11, 51, 53, 56, 90, 132, 158, 177, 183, 194, 216, 249

Mithras, 156

Monday, 20

money, 14–15, 23, 88, 94, 108–109, 145, 147, 151, 166, 168

Moon, 4, 6, 19–24, 29, 32–35, 49, 54, 61, 72–73, 75–76, 82–83, 85, 97, 101, 104, 110, 114, 119–121, 123, 125, 128–129, 147, 152, 155–156, 159, 161, 173, 177–178, 184, 191, 198, 201, 207–208, 216, 220–221, 223–226

    Full, 4, 32, 36, 56, 99, 121, 123, 178, 215–216, 223, 225, 240

    New, 3, 16, 25, 32, 38, 54, 85, 95–96, 112, 114, 125, 161, 178, 208–209, 214, 216, 221, 232, 243

    phases, 32, 120, 221, 226

    planting by, 32, 35, 178, 208, 220–221

    Waning, 20, 32, 35, 54, 72, 75–76, 114, 156, 221, 223

    Waxing, 6, 20, 23, 32, 49, 61, 72, 85, 97, 104, 129, 152, 178, 201, 220

Moon Sign Book, 4, 23

mortar and pestle, 8–9, 55, 120

mountain ash, 194, 219

mugwort, 45, 51, 55–56, 61–62, 64, 66–67, 77, 90, 132, 178, 209, 214, 234, 238

mullein, 51, 91, 131–132, 179, 232

musk, 61, 82, 103, 105–107, 112

myrrh, 50, 73–74, 92, 103, 112, 124, 126–127, 151, 179

myrtle, 82–85, 92, 180–181

names of herbs, magical, 231–232

Narcissus, 74, 112

nasturtiums, 222

neroli, 112

nettle, 91, 131, 181

new-mown hay, 112

nightmares, 138, 144, 169, 202, 205

north, 4, 24, 52, 107, 152, 178, 215–217, 219, 244

North Wind, 107

nudity, 27–28

numerology, 28

nutmeg, 60–61, 90, 113, 128, 181

nuts, 84–85, 164, 182, 190–191

oak, 6, 26, 53, 75, 91, 96, 183–184, 223, 247–249

oils, magical, 99, 105, 107, 143

olive oil, 10, 72, 101, 104

Olwen, 139

onion, 76, 78, 184, 214, 223

orange sweet, 185
   blossom, 108, 113, 151, 222
orris, 66, 82–83, 92, 104, 113, 123,
      126, 128, 161, 185, 233
Osiris, 136, 170

paeon, 187
Pan, 64, 190
pansy, 92, 186, 233
parsley, 103, 133, 154, 173, 215,
      233, 241, 246
partnerships, 21, 89
passion, 10, 105, 107, 110, 132,
      148, 151, 161, 186
past lives, recalling, 111
patchouli, 90, 103–104, 106, 113,
      129, 186
peace, 10, 105, 108–113, 116, 177
pendulum, 66, 209
pennyroyal, 77, 91, 187
pentagram, 43, 219
peony, 51, 91, 113, 187, 221
pepper, 91, 188, 210, 223
peppermint, 77, 90, 97, 113, 126,
      189, 214
periwinkle, 51, 83, 92, 189, 214,
      234
Persephone, 156, 207
physical strength, 21
pimpernel, 51, 90, 132, 190, 245
pimples, 72, 75
pine, 6, 26, 90, 124, 190–191
   cone, 6, 120, 190
pink, 10, 82–84, 104, 163
pins, 11, 29, 147
planetary incense, 128
Plutarch, 125
Pluto, 156
polarity, 88
poison, 165, 178
   protection against, 78, 105, 140,
      143, 146, 195
politics, 21
pomegranate, 84
poplar, 26

poppet, 43, 114, 139, 181
poppy, 67, 84, 92, 128, 191
Poseidon, 140
power, 5, 8, 14, 17, 19–21, 24–26,
      28–29, 33, 40–41, 69–70, 79,
      94, 96, 105, 109, 115–116,
      119, 121, 127–128, 148–149,
      151, 154, 158–159, 163,
      166–168, 170, 172, 179, 182,
      185–186, 188, 189–190, 192,
      198–201, 203–204, 206, 208,
      210, 232
primrose, 91, 192, 233
promotions, 21, 88
prosperity, 6, 10, 15, 20, 23, 94,
      100, 108, 110, 112, 128, 142,
      145, 147, 151, 166–168,
      170–171, 191, 197
   incense, 10, 21, 24, 27, 40, 50,
      55–56, 60–62, 64, 73, 82,
      99, 109, 113, 119–129,
      149, 151, 160–161, 194,
      196, 201–202, 239
   sachet, 15, 26–27, 40, 44, 51–53,
      75, 77–79, 82–85, 131,
      142, 148, 151, 167, 172,
      185, 191, 194, 204, 206
prostitutes, 108, 111
protection, 6, 20, 43, 49–57, 78, 89,
      103, 105, 109, 112, 114–115,
      122–123, 131, 136, 138,
      140–146, 148–152, 154–157,
      160–165, 167, 169–172, 174,
      176–181, 183–184, 187–190,
      192–195, 197–199, 201, 205,
      209, 222–223
protection incense, 123
pruning, 224
psychic powers, 59, 68, 107–108,
      111, 116, 137
purification, 6–7, 26–27, 54–56,
      104, 108, 110, 112, 121–122,
      138–139, 142–146, 151,
      157–158, 161, 169, 172–173,
      180, 184, 189–190, 193,
      195–196, 198–199, 202,
      204–205, 208

purple, 10, 143, 152, 166
purslane, 85

Ra, 161, 180
rain, 29, 160, 165–166, 222
raisins, 125–126
rape, 132, 165
recuperation, 89, 110, 194
red, 7, 10–11, 35, 49, 51–53, 56,
        72, 78, 84, 95, 106, 114, 129,
        137, 144, 149, 153, 159,
        163–164, 192–193, 195, 198,
        222–223, 239, 247
repetition, 29, 42, 52
Rhea, 183
rheumatism, 182, 207
ritual, 14–15, 18, 23, 27, 43–44,
        49, 55, 65, 70, 75, 82, 104,
        108–109, 112, 120, 124, 139,
        153, 156, 180, 183, 194,
        222–223
river, 95–96, 203, 208
robe, 7, 27–28, 33, 54
Rome, 67
roots, 19, 32, 35–36, 51, 140,
        145–147, 174, 184, 188, 199,
        221–222, 225, 231
rose, 36, 50–51, 67, 73, 82, 84, 92,
        105–107, 113–114, 124,
        127–129, 150, 174, 192–193
rose geranium, 50–51, 105, 114
rosemary, 10–11, 25–26, 49–51,
        55–56, 64, 72, 74, 84, 91,
        105, 114, 123, 126–127, 147,
        172, 176, 188, 193–194, 214,
        225, 232, 246
rowan, 6, 51, 53–54, 91, 194–195,
        234, 247
rue, 11, 49, 51, 56, 74–75, 79, 85,
        91, 114–115, 131–133, 147,
        195, 214–215, 224, 246

sachets, 11, 17, 26, 28, 49, 51, 66,
        82–83, 85, 95–96, 141–143,
        146, 148, 150, 153–154, 157,
        161–163, 165–166, 168–169,
        171–172, 174–175, 177, 181,
        185, 193–194, 196–197, 200,
        203, 205, 210, 213
    divinatory, 60, 108, 144, 182,
        209, 236
    fertility, 6, 10, 20, 27, 84–85,
        88, 144, 155–156,
        163–164, 174, 180,
        182–183, 190–192, 201,
        206–207, 215
    healing, 6, 10, 21, 43, 69–79,
        89, 95, 109–111, 114–116,
        137, 139–140, 142–143,
        151, 153–155, 159, 163,
        165, 168, 172, 180, 182,
        184, 189, 193–198, 200,
        206–208, 214, 227
    love, 6, 10, 14, 18, 20–21, 25,
        27, 34, 81–85, 89, 96,
        104–105, 107–110, 113,
        116, 129, 138–139,
        141–142, 148, 150–151,
        154–155, 157–158,
        160–161, 163, 166,
        169–177, 180–182,
        185–187, 192–193, 196,
        200, 203–206, 210, 214,
        227, 233, 238–239
    protective, 49–54, 56–57, 105,
        108–110, 113–115, 137,
        141, 147, 153, 161–162,
        167, 169, 173–174, 176,
        178, 184, 188, 194, 199
saffron, 73–74, 91, 115, 133, 196
sage, 74, 90, 96, 196, 214–215,
        246, 249
St. John's wort, 45, 51, 55, 91, 197,
        247, 250
salt, 10, 26, 49, 99, 114
Saturn, 21–22, 128, 139, 141, 144,
        154, 156, 160, 166, 170, 179,
        186, 198–199
Samhain, 43, 110, 139, 164, 209

sand, 7, 10

sandalwood, 7, 61, 66, 72, 74–75, 90, 103, 109, 115, 123–124, 127, 129, 136, 198

Saturday, 21

Saturn, 21–22, 128, 139, 141, 144, 154, 156, 160, 166, 170, 179, 186, 198–199

satyr oil, 106

scent, 26, 85, 99–100, 102, 105–106, 108, 110, 112–113, 115, 119, 121, 126, 131, 186

scrying, 61, 64, 178

scrying incense, 61, 64

sea, 10, 21, 26, 49, 132, 140, 173, 193, 232

second sight, 59–61, 115, 176

sesame, 116

sexuality, 84

silver, 4, 53, 113, 138

simples, 64

sleep, 20, 66–67, 111, 113, 125, 133, 144, 147–148, 168, 172–173, 193, 234–235, 238, 249

slippery elm, 90, 198

snakes, 153, 163, 246

snapdragon, 35, 51, 132, 199

Solomon's seal, 128, 199

Somnos, 191

sorrell, 76

south, 5, 107, 132, 215, 217, 219

South Wind, 107

southernwood, 84, 233

spearmint, 74, 90, 200

spirits, 27, 70, 89, 93–95, 97, 100, 107, 109–111, 141, 150–151, 162, 171, 197, 209

spikenard, 116

star anise, 66, 92, 200

storing, 8, 10, 16, 31, 37–38, 41, 50, 73, 75, 93, 97, 99–101, 103, 105, 120, 122, 152, 174, 193, 220

storms, to prevent, 69, 77–78, 132–133, 144, 149, 152, 162, 178, 182, 187
  to stop, 153, 172, 188, 194, 198, 237

strawberry leaves, 82

study incense, 126

substitutions, 29, 52, 104, 174, 179, 219

success incense,123

sweet pea, 116

sulphur

Sun, 20–22, 24, 29, 33–34, 36, 73, 93, 101, 110, 119, 125, 128, 136–137, 140, 142–143, 147, 149–150, 152–153, 159–160, 164–165, 171, 173, 175–177, 180, 183, 185–187, 193–197, 201, 206, 220, 225–226

Sunday, 20

sunflower, 201, 241

tarragon, 51, 233

tansy, 82, 210

teaching, 21, 89

thief, 165, 174

thistle, 78–79, 91, 201

Thor, 140, 164, 183, 194, 205

thorn, 136, 163, 247

Thursday, 21, 23, 129, 151

thyme, 26, 64, 90, 133, 202

ti, 132

toad, 225

tobacco, 71, 91, 97, 165, 178, 202–203

tools, 3–11, 16, 19, 33, 59, 82–85, 87, 96–97, 110, 116, 119, 180

tonka beans, 84, 201, 203

tormentil, 84

travel, 14, 32, 78, 89

trefoil, 49, 51, 152

trees, 6, 18, 25, 65, 133, 182–183, 207, 213, 215–216, 219, 221, 223, 225, 227, 231

tuberose, 116, 233

Tuesday, 21, 106

unicorn, 133, 234

universal fluid condenser, 96

valerian, 26, 82, 85, 203–204, 233
vampires, 76
vanilla, 91, 106, 116, 151, 204
Venus, 20–22, 105–106, 128,
        137–139, 146, 149, 155, 158,
        164, 169, 172, 175, 178, 180,
        185, 187, 189–190, 192,
        199–200, 202–203, 205–206,
        210
vervain, 11, 26, 51, 56, 82, 84, 91,
        102–103, 116, 124, 127, 132,
        158, 205, 214, 222, 226, 233,
        245
vibrations, 15, 19, 25, 39, 41, 49,
        54, 60, 75, 99–100, 107,
        109–110, 113–114, 119, 151,
        159, 161, 176–177, 220
victory, 132, 209
violet, 74, 84, 92, 96, 116, 186,
        189, 206, 234
Vishnu, 142
vision incense, 62, 239
visualization, 17, 94, 96, 115, 214, 222
vitality, 10

walnut, 182, 206–207
wand, 6–8, 94, 208
war, 21, 76, 89, 197
warts, 70, 72, 75, 139
water element, 139–140, 146–149,
        155, 158, 161, 163, 165–166,
        168–170, 173, 177, 180,
        185–186, 189, 191–192, 200,
        203–207, 210
water spring, 4, 11, 62–63, 73, 94,
        97, 195, 222
weariness, 132, 187
Wednesday, 21, 61–62
west, 5, 95, 107, 215, 217, 219,
        225, 244
West Wind, 65, 107, 137, 145, 217,
        219, 227
white, 3, 5, 10, 24, 26–27, 33, 49,
        51, 53–55, 60–61, 78, 84, 95,
        121, 125–126, 145, 163, 168,
        191, 198, 207, 234

willow, 6, 92, 140, 207–208, 215,
        219, 234
wind, 65, 107, 137, 145, 217, 219,
        227
wine, 7, 35, 125–126, 139,
        184–185, 209
wisdom, 109, 123, 151, 164, 182,
        213
wishing magic, 6
wisteria, 117
Witch, 14, 31, 33, 39–42, 44, 60,
        62, 70, 73, 105, 135–210, 213,
        220, 223, 225, 227, 232,
        234–236, 238, 240, 245
Witches sight incense, 61
Witches sight oil, 60
Woden, 140
woodruff, 132, 208, 233
world leaders, 21
wormwood, 64, 90, 209, 214, 232
        healing, 6, 10, 21, 43, 69–79,
                89, 95, 109–111,
                114–116, 137, 139–140,
                142–143, 151, 153–155,
                159, 163, 165, 168, 172,
                180, 182, 184, 189,
                193–198, 200, 206–208,
                214, 227
        protection against, 78, 105, 140,
                143, 146, 195
wounds, 72–75, 78–79, 89, 178, 210
wreath, 56–57, 194
writing, 89

yarrow, 11, 34, 36, 55, 64–65, 82,
        84–85, 92, 105, 131, 210,
        214, 233–234, 246
yellow, 7, 10, 60, 64, 66, 84, 140,
        191, 198
yew, 215
ylang-ylang, 106, 117
Yule, 124

Zeus, 183

The Complete Book of Incense, Oils and Brews

Scott Cunningham

For centuries, the composition of incenses, the blending of oils, and the mixing of herbs have been used by people to create positive changes in their lives.

With this book, the curtains of secrecy have been drawn back, providing you with practical, easy-to-understand information that will allow you to practice these methods of magical cookery. There is no special, costly equipment to buy, and ingredients are usually easy to find.

The book also includes detailed information on a wide variety of herbs, sources for purchasing ingredients, substitutions for hard-to-find herbs, a glossary, and a chapter on creating your own magical recipes.

0-87542-128-8
288 pp., 6 x 9, illus.   **$16.95**
Also Available in Spanish

Earth Power

Techniques of Natural Magic

SCOTT CUNNINGHAM

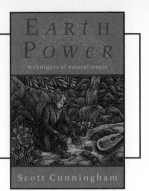

Magick is the art of working with the forces of nature to bring about necessary and desired changes. The forces of nature—expressed through Earth, Air, Fire, and Water—are our "spiritual ancestors" who paved the way for our emergence from the prehistoric seas of creation.

Attuning to and working with these energies in magick not only lends you the power to effect changes in your life, it also allows you to sense your own place in the larger scheme of nature. Using the "Old Ways" enables you to live a better life and to deepen your understanding of the world.

The tools and powers of magick are around you, waiting to be grasped and used. This book gives you the means to put magick into your life, shows you how to make and use the tools, and gives you spells for every purpose.

0-87542-121-0
176 pp., 5 ¼ x 8, illus.   **$11.95**